About the Author

Regina Junk is an average suburban mom who loves hiking and spending time with her children. She enjoys the outdoors and walking her dogs. You can usually find her in the mountains or on a beach somewhere.

Between Two Jags:
My Air Force Affair

Regina Junk

Between Two Jags:
My Air Force Affair

Olympia Publishers
London

www.olympiapublishers.com
OLYMPIA PAPERBACK EDITION

A CIP catalogue record for this title is
available from the British Library.

ISBN: 978-1-80439-439-7

This book is a memoir. It reflects the author's present recollections of
experiences over time. Some names and characteristics have been changed,
some events have been compressed, other events dramatized, and some
dialogue has been recreated.

First Published in 2024

Olympia Publishers
Tallis House
2 Tallis Street
London
EC4Y 0AB
Printed in Great Britain

Dedication

For Rebecca, Trista, and Eve, may you have a life filled with what the universe feels you deserve; may someone care about your feelings like you did for others; and I hope your children treat you as well as you treated others and your parents, mostly our husbands.

Acknowledgements

Raven, you have been amazing through the years. Thank you for being the sun on my face. To the rest of my kids, I couldn't have gotten through all of this without you all. I love you so much!

Just when I thought I had it all figured out and the world couldn't be any brighter, things went dark. Dark as in controlling and abusive. How did I end up here, and how was I going to get out unscathed? They seemed normal, but behind closed doors, after they began to relax, the real people came out, and there was no escape and no turning back. I had no idea how to cope or handle them. What happened next blindsided even me and turned me into a person I didn't recognize.

PROLOGUE

I love being a team mom. Going to the gym and watching my daughter train was one of the greatest joys of my life. It was a day like any other at the gym. Girls showed up and began to get ready for warmups. That's when they walked in, with their daughters trailing behind them. You could clearly see they were new to the area and were military. Two things we had in common, military and gym. But this was just the beginning of a friendship that turned dark and seductive. Lines were crossed, trust was broken, and rules did not exist.

While She was deployed

Her instructions to him, keep my friendships alive while I'm gone. Spend time with her and keep her close.

This part of our relationship was kind of a blur. There are a few key things that truly stand out during this time. The emails and calls from her were usually short but very heartfelt. She seemed to genuinely be concerned with how I was and how the man I was living with was treating me. I should have seen this as a grooming technique, but my eyes and my mind refused to see it as such. I literally felt she was being a true friend and wanting to keep up with and give advice about my life.

She would call and ask questions about the things he would say to me and relay them to her husband. I should have seen the game they were beginning to play with my life, and I should have run. Maybe a part of me did see it and just didn't care. Whatever the reason, they knew exactly how to get to me and used the love I had for my daughter to get what they wanted.

Keeping up with her demands, he would talk to me at the gym about meets, and hotel stays. Since our girls were friends, our conversations were usually about them and what they were doing. Just proud parents watching their young ladies grow and become amazing athletes. He and I really didn't talk much and breaking the ice between us looked like it was going to be more difficult than either of us imagined.

Our first adventure together was to a gymnastics meet. I was nervous because I really didn't know him, and I pretty much gave all my attention to the kids on the ride. Five hours in a vehicle is a very long time to listen to the voices in your head tell you what to say and then tell you it sounds dumb. By the time we arrived at the hotel I was mentally exhausted and ready to just relax.

He and I unloaded the kid's stuff and ours for the doorman to load on the cart. He said he was going to park and meet me in the room. He handed me the keys and tip money and walked away.

A lady came up and grabbed our cart and escorted us to the elevator. When she pushed the buttons, she had to use our room key to make the elevator activate. I then panicked. He was parking, I had all the room keys and didn't know what to do. When I asked her about it, she confirmed it took a key to activate the elevator. I told her he was parking and asked how he would get to the room. She asked if I was talking about my husband and without thought I replied yes. Then an abrupt no came out followed by telling her he was my best friend's husband. I continued to dig myself into a hole of embarrassment as all the kids were laughing. Telling her it was fine because my best friend was deployed to explaining to her she knew we were at the hotel together. I seriously wanted to crawl into a hole at this point.

By the time he got to the room, our escort was fuming. He had no idea what had happened, but the kids had no problem letting him know he just got married in the elevator and missed the whole ceremony. It became kind of a joke that has been going on since that day.

The first thing he did was email his wife to tell her he had another wife. I was thinking to myself as he was sending it about how angry she was going to be and how this friendship that had started before she left was going to end quickly. My heart was racing, and I was starting to feel a bit sick to my stomach.

The next thing I knew, she was calling. I could hear her laughing and asking him when he decided she needed a sister wife. Wait, she wasn't mad? As the call went on, I could hear more and more excitement in her voice. She seemed thrilled to have a sister wife. I was so confused. Thinking back, was this her plan all along? To rope me in as family?

The weekend was great. We all had a lot of fun, and the ride back wasn't bad at all. He and I talked about meets and kids and all kinds of things we like to do. It was obvious his kids were very important to him. That was something we had in common, our kids and our love for our kids. It was nice to see a man love his kids so much.

SPRING BREAK

Even though my "sister wife" was deployed, she had training she had to attend stateside. It just happened to be at the beach, and she wanted to make sure "our" husband talked me into going with him when he went to see her with their girls.

Sister wife had sent several emails and made several calls to try to talk me into the trip. I really wanted to go. I loved the beach, and I knew my girls could use some relaxation time.

I finally caved and decided to go. What could be so bad? Over ten hours in a car with a man I barely know sounded fantastic. I really hope you can sense the sarcasm there.

After about three hours, I began to wonder if our Husband was going to talk or turn the radio on. It was quiet, other than a few giggles from the back of the car. It was our Husband, five girls and me in the car and the girls all had earbuds in.

I finally asked him if he ever listened to the radio. He said if I was bored, we could talk. He then began to ask me all kinds of questions about myself and my life.

It was hours and hours of Q & A. He seemed genuinely interested in what I was saying, and he began to talk about himself. I learned a lot about him on the way to the beach. Things like, where he was from, what his parents did for a living, he had a sister, he met sister wife at college, they married because he knocked her up, you know things everyone should know, I guess.

I was thankful when we arrived and were able to settle in. We were staying about five miles from where my sister wife was staying. It was late and I was ready to just go to bed.

The first day was smooth, we went to the beach and hung out by the pool at sister's hotel. All the girls got along, and it seemed as if this was going to be a really nice trip.

Our Husband's family showed up for some family time. While they were doing family time, I took my girls and went to the beach. We were also able to get some shopping done while everyone else was doing whatever it was they did during family time.

Towards the end of the week, we all went to play mini golf together. I should have seen some serious red flags here but again I overlooked it all.

While we were playing, their youngest, Eve, got angry over not making the ball in and threw her club across the golf area. Our Husband also got angry and threw his because Eve was angry. Sister wife stomped her feet like a toddler and began to scream.

I looked at my girls with serious confusion. What had just happened? Eve started screaming at sister and from there I really cannot tell you what happened. I just knew I wanted out of there and was looking for the nearest exit.

We all left the next day. The ride home was different. I looked at our Husband differently because of his reactions to sister and Eve. How could he have lost his cool so fast? Was it because sister was there? I had seen Eve act up before, but his reaction was very different this time.

Our Husband broke the ice and started talking to me about two hours into the car ride. He talked about all the things he wanted to do over the summer with all the kids and how he wanted me and my girls to also go. This made me happy. He wanted to spend time with us.

At this point it seemed like the season for the kids flew by. With the ending of the season also came the end of the school year and time for summer fun. I wasn't ready for what the summer was going to bring or what it was going to lead to. All I knew, the kids were going to have a great time and I was all about bringing my actual sister (Karma) with me.

SUMMER

Now with summer training happening, the kids were at the gym even more. At this time, the sister-wife thing had really gotten a lot of talk and laughs. It was interesting and sometimes caused a huge argument between me and the guy I was living with. I mean, I can see why I don't think I would have appreciated someone calling my significant other anything but a friend.

When talking to my sister wife about this she continued to tell me how bad he was for me and how I should just spend the summer with our Husband. Again, I felt as if this was just a silly thing that we were joking about and not her grooming techniques. Looking back, I can't help but question if he was in on it from the very beginning.

It started out as small local trips to a bigger city near us. With all our younger kids loaded up we headed to the zoo. This was the day I began to see more of their family dynamics and how they interacted with each other and with friends. There were red flags and I looked right past them. The only thing that mattered to me was that my girls were having a good time. His girls, fighting the whole time.

One in particular, (Eve) seemed to demand most of the attention and most of the items in the gift shops. There was something there with her but at this point I hadn't known them long enough to put my finger on it.

The day at the zoo had ended and we were all so tired. On the ride back to our small town our Husband began to talk to me about other places we could go. As we talked, we compiled a mental list of places we felt the kids would enjoy close to home but still entertaining.

Our next adventure was a bit chaotic. By this time our Husband invited my boyfriend and another mom from the gym and her kids. We were all friends who never really had difficulty having a good time together. This is the day things began to get a little bit uncomfortable. The other mom had announced she was going to be wife number three and he was going to be a communal Husband.

What was she thinking? Did she think there wasn't going to be any blowback from this? That statement set in motion events I could have never predicted which I will get to later.

The only good thing that came from a third wife was my boyfriend decided we were all just joking, and it really wasn't a thing. Something I had been telling him all along. Now, my hopes of him being more agreeable with the trips we were planning for the rest of the summer had gone up.

We had a ton of fun over the next several weeks. We took several day trips to various places with the kids. Sometimes Karma went us or his "third" wife and her kids. Other times it was just me, our Husband and all the kids.

My boyfriend (let's call him Kane) was too busy working to take time off even with his six weeks of vacation sitting there. This became what I now see as a weapon my sister wife used to put distance between me and Kane. I would hear stories about how our Husband would take time to spend with me and the kids and how a man in my house who claimed to love me couldn't take an afternoon to go to the park. The more she talked the more I felt unloved.

While she was tearing Kane down to just a person living in

the same space, she was also telling me how much she valued me and my friendship. I tried very hard to find something she and I had in common, but our Husband seemed to be the only thing we had in common. She assured me almost daily that I was loved and wanted in her life and our husband's life. The more I heard it the more I believed it.

Then came a proposal for a longer trip. Some place where we could camp, and the kids could enjoy the outdoors. We all did some research and came up with an amusement park in a neighboring state. Of course, being gone for several days I felt taking Karma was a good idea. I was hoping it would keep Kane from flipping out over nothing.

It was set and we were all on our way. The trip there was just as fun as being there in my opinion. Just being around people who seemed to care and seeing my kids have a good time was enough to fill my heart with all kinds of love.

With park passes in hand we were off to the park on day two. Roller coasters and water rides and all kinds of games. Then it happened. His youngest, Eve, was literally throwing a fit. I had no idea a kid this old would throw a toddler size tantrum… and in public!

As she got louder and louder, I watched him slowly walk over to her and calmly talk to her. She was putting up a fight, but he continued to talk to her and calm her down. Watching this interaction hit me hard, in a way I never thought anything would ever hit me again. That very moment, I fell in love with our Husband.

I had to physically turn my back to him. I couldn't let him see my face because I knew he would see it. Karma noticed my breathing had picked up and asked me if I was OK. I had to immediately take an inventory of all my external physical attributes. Not just my breathing which had become rapid and heavy, but my hands began to shake. Was my face flush? Was I making it too obvious I wasn't looking in his direction? Did he already notice? I was in a complete panic.

About the time I felt faint from all my panic symptoms he put his hand on my shoulder. The electric bolt that went through my body and straight to my Netherlands was completely unexpected. Did that just happen? My whole mind and body felt weak and confused by all my involuntary responses. Obviously, I jumped as I spun around trying to think of what I was going to say. Just as our eyes met, he motioned for me to sit with him on the ride. I let out a sigh as my sister laughed because she thought he scared me.

As we pulled the safety bar down on the ride I felt as if I had dodged a bullet. He put his hand on my leg and again that bolt hit me. All I could think at that point was how I wanted to kiss him and feel his breath on my skin. He looked at me and smiled in a way I hadn't seen before. Did he know? Could he see it on my face? Feel it in my breathing? Maybe he could see how my heart was about to beat right out of my chest.

When the ride was over it was right back to running to the next ride. It seemed everyone was the same as they were ten minutes before. Everyone except me, I was different. I had felt something, something hadn't felt since my husband had died years before. Love, actual real, no conditions, no exceptions, no anything other than just love.

The rest of the day I tried to not make eye contact and not be obvious about it. I kept telling myself how wrong my feelings were and how much I hated having them. I also came to the reality they weren't going away anytime soon.

That night, as we all went to bed, Karma broke the silence

with a slight whisper.

Her one sentence, "You think I didn't see that but, I saw that."

Now my body was paralyzed with fear. I didn't have to ask her what she saw because I already knew. That means, he must know. He had to know. How could he not?

What excuse could I find to divert the conversation if he brings it up? Is he going to tell sister wife? Did any of the kids notice? How was I going to be able to handle the ride home with all this going through my head and my body?

Thankfully the girls were all laughing and talking the whole ride back. There was no time to think about or even better, talk about what had happened at the park. Karma never said a word, I was very thankful for her silence.

RETURNING TO EVERYDAY LIFE

Back home from our short getaway, things began to go back to normal. Girls were back in the gym; I was back to running them everywhere and our Husband was back to work. Kane was the same guy I had left there days before, angry all the time about something someone did and cursing.

My sister wife was excited to get all the pictures we sent her while we were gone. She boasted about how she knew I would have a blast on the trip and how the kids would enjoy the time away from the gym. She talked a lot about how handsome our Husband was and how she knew we would get along. She called me the female version of our Husband. We all laughed probably because it was mostly true.

A few weeks later while waiting for the girls to finish at the gym, our Husband shows up. He looks a bit sad, but I wasn't going to pressure him for what was wrong. Then, with a huge sigh, he announced they were moving.

I could feel my chest get tight and my eyes start to water. I knew this day would come because of the military but I hadn't imagined it would happen so soon. Had we already known each other for two years? Was this life telling me I was wrong for having feelings? Was I being punished?

When I finally was able to stop my head from spinning, I turned to him and asked how long before they leave. I'm not sure if my mind refused to hear what he was saying or if I clearly blacked out. I could see his mouth moving but there were no words. I didn't say anything back, I just stood there.

The movers came and packed up all the belongings they had. Our Husband was sending houses to my text to see what I thought of them. After narrowing it down to two, it was weird that we all had agreed on the same house.

I received a call from sister wife after the purchase to make sure I liked the house. Why did it matter? They were leaving and he was taking my heart with him. She made it clear there was an extra room reserved for me at the house for frequent visits or extended visits. But my heart was still breaking.

She began to tell me the only thing Kane would miss was the fact that I was his mother. I ordered his medications, did the laundry, shopped, cooked and ran the entire house without help and she made it clear he wouldn't miss me he would miss the slave he has in the house taking care of things.

As much as her words hurt, I began to realize she was probably right. Did I not see it before? How could I not see it? This made our Husband leaving even worse.

This is about the time the third wife chimed in and told me it would be fine. She knew I was in love with him, and she had a lot to say about it. She began to ask questions about the couple and how I would even fit into the relationship. She questioned what if anything they saw in each other. She asked me if they had anything in common. I had zero answers to the questions and all I cared was that he was leaving, and she was deployed, and I was going to be alone...with Kane.

The next few days were gut wrenching. It was like waiting for something to explode and rip my body apart. How did I let myself get to this place? That seemed to be a question I asked myself often. I knew the leaving day was coming and the closer it got the less I was able to function.

The third wife tried to comfort me. She talked about sister wife like she was nothing but weird and awkward. Telling me she had no idea how our Husband related to her or how anyone could relate to her.

Third wife trashed sister wife so often and with such distaste for her I should have seen what later came. I didn't, probably because I was overwhelmed with heartbreak.

MISERY & SOLITUDE

I woke up early, made coffee and sat on the couch to look through all the social media I follow. I was reading some silly memes one of my friends posted and then it hit me. Today was the day. Our Husband is leaving.

Panic started to set in along with pain and sadness. I felt lost and I couldn't breathe. What was I going to do? How was I going to hide this from not just Kane but everyone in my life? I had to stop thinking about it. I had to get out of my own head. I decided a walk was what I needed before everyone got out of bed.

When I returned to the house, my kids were up. One had gotten a text letting her know our Husband and the girls were on the way to the house to say the typical military "see ya later."

A lump formed in my throat. I was not going to make it through this today without tears and emotions I so desperately needed to hide. I went into the bathroom to wash my face and try to look somewhat presentable. No amount of water or soap could wash the sadness off my face. He was going to see it and so was the rest of the world.

As they pulled up in front of the house the kids were already crying. They were the best of friends and had spent so much time together. This could work out to my advantage. My kid cries, I cry. Made sense to me and I was hoping it would to everyone else.

As he got out and walked towards me it was like someone opened the floodgates of my tear ducts. I could not stop crying.

What is wrong with me? How was he going to react seeing all these tears? What was he going to think? When I finally looked up, a bit of shock and relief hit me. Was he also crying? Are those tears on his face? Did he feel the same? I wasn't about to ask him and even if I wanted to, all I could do was stand there.

I was frozen in this state of sadness and crying in my front yard. He was walking towards me with his eyes locked on mine. My breathing picked up and I could feel my body start to weaken. How will I handle this not just today but for the days coming?

When he finally stood in front of me, he embraced me with such force I felt my body fall into his. I could feel his heartbeat against my chest. I could feel my body trembling as his warm breath hit my neck. I'm getting hot and I have goosebumps traveling down my neck to my inner thigh.

For a few moments I let my mind wonder what it would be like for him to touch my bare skin. Was he a satisfying love maker or was he selfish? I imagined what it would feel like for his tongue to caress my lips just before a long seductive kiss.

I must have started breathing heavily as the thoughts ran through my mind. He let go and stepped back. I tried to smile as he asked if I was OK. Yep, he noticed. As I leaned in to tell him how difficult this was all I could get out was "I feel like you are taking half of my heart with you."

I expected a reaction of shock or confusion. He reached down and grabbed my hand and whispered, "I feel like I'm leaving half of my heart here."

What just happened? Did he just? My head is spinning, and I feel like I'm spiraling into a hole of darkness. Am I breathing?

He squeezed my hand and smiled as he handed me an envelope. He asked that I wait until later to open it as he hugged me one last time. Watching them drive away, a sadness came over me I hadn't felt in years.

I walked into the house holding the red envelope. I felt alone and empty. When I opened it, tears began to fall. Reading it was even more difficult. His words hand-written in the card were very personal and heartfelt. My heart was broken.

VISITING THE NEW PLACE

My sister wife and our Husband made it clear the new place was open for visits anytime I felt like going. It didn't take long for me to load up the car, kids (Raven and Koi) and my sisters Karma and Jade (I couldn't leave her out) and head south.

It seemed like it took forever to get there. Why did we have to live so far apart? Excitement built as we crossed the bridge, I could smell the salt in the air. We were so close, and I was so ready to see his face.

Pulling into the driveway my hands began to shake. The front door opened and there she was, my sister wife. She was obviously excited to see us. She was an only child and she had adopted my actual sisters as her own. She was happy to have an extended family.

Then, our Husband came out. Chills ran down my back and my breathing increased. I could feel parts of my body warm just from the sight of him. He hugged me and sent my insides into convulsions.

With Jade and Karma there I knew I was going to have to keep my distance from him. They were able to spot a difference in me from a mile away and that was the last thing I wanted.

While my sister wife was busy trying to be the center of attention, our Husband and I would go for walks around the neighborhood or down to the mailbox. We did a lot of talking and I realized not only did I feel like he had my heart but also my mind. He was my best friend.

We spent the week sight-seeing and checking out local places of interest. I think playing on the beach was the best. The girls were glad to see each-other and it seemed as if everyone was happy.

Seemed is a good word for what you would have noticed on the outside. My sister wife eventually began to show what she was really like and part of that scared me. The other part of me felt the need to help her. After all, I wanted our Husband to be happy and if she was happy, it seemed he was happy.

This is when I began to watch her, not like what she did on a daily basis but how she acted and reacted to all situations that were presented to her. I studied her to see what made her tick and what set her off. The list of setting her off was much longer than any other list I was able to compile.

Making him happy was going to be an uphill battle if I couldn't figure out what she was missing and how I could make it better for her. She had holes in her life that were never filled, and I wasn't sure if I would be able to figure out what was missing and how to fill them.

I soon figured out some of her needs. The need for affirmation and praise were high on the list. Being the center of attention was also way up there. I watched her beam with pride if one of the girls did something great but it wasn't pride for the girls, it was pride for the fact she gave birth to them and because of her they were doing great things. Sister wife's need for taking credit for all things good was very evident.

If there was any type of success, she would find a way to make sure it only happened because of her. This meant I needed to make sure all positive things that occurred were directly related to something she had done or an idea she had developed. I could do this. I will do this. Our Husband needed this in order to keep peace in the house. A sacrifice I was willing to make.

This visit was fun, and we all enjoyed ourselves. My sisters were very happy to be able to kick back and relax. Mostly away from the house because of the conflict sister wife had with mostly our Husband and their youngest child Eve.

On leaving day I again felt very sad to be leaving him, but I knew I would be back, and I made sure to let him know it wasn't going to be long.

TIME BETWEEN VISITS

After my first visit I was completely engulfed with him. I was having a hard time not thinking about him even when things were crazy at home.

Kane wasn't happy when I arrived home and all I could talk about was things our Husband and I did when everyone else was busy. He didn't seem to understand how easy it was to talk to our Husband and how he and I could be so close. I just had a connection, and it was one I couldn't explain.

Just when I thought things couldn't get any more confusing, my phone rang. It was our husband. What started out as a casual conversation about daily life turned into one of the most erotic conversations I have ever had.

Obviously, we both cleared the air about our feelings for one another. We also agreed that my sister wife would have to be a part of the relationship. So many details were discussed in this conversation on his end there was no way I was going to be able to remember them all.

One of the things I do remember is listening to him tell me how he felt about me and most of the conversation was me listening. I would talk when he asked a question or was attempting to verify my feelings for him. He was very open about how he felt both mentally and physically. This is where our relationship went from sweet and innocent to seductive and sultry.

Did my sister wife know what he was up to? Did she put him

up to it? As with most things that went on between us, I feel like she had to know, and he just didn't tell me. Maybe she was coaching him on what to say and what to do to lure me into their lives.

Our phone calls became more than calls to check on one another. His eagerness to show me how I turned him on was not muted. He would talk about stroking his cock as he talked to me. How he looked at my pictures as he would masturbate and cum all over himself.

Sister wife was still deployed, and I was states away I saw no harm in pleasing our Husband in this way. I did at times feel bad when I was so tense and hungry for a good fucking and went to Kane for my release. I also felt bad for imagining it was our Husband instead of Kane, but I couldn't help myself. My mind and my heart were somewhere else and with someone else.

I know Kane picked up on how my feelings were different than before. He questioned me but I blew them off like he was imagining things. I wasn't sure how long I could keep this up, but I was going to try.

I felt terrible hiding things from Kane. In my defense, he was loud and rude and was constantly calling me names. My sister wife would remind me of this all the time. She would talk about how what happens to Kane would be because he caused it himself, and he will get what he deserved in the end. She sounded a bit vindictive, but I soon put it out of my mind.

Our Husband would send videos of himself stroking his cock and calling my name. It was very erotic to see him looking into the camera, like he was looking right at me and not his phone. His dick swollen and ready to explode, moaning as if I was the one stroking him.

I could always tell when he was about to cum, his breathing

36

and moaning would get faster and louder. It didn't matter if we were on FaceTime or it was a video sent to me, he still called my name as he came all over his hand and stomach.

Weeks of FaceTime and videos had me so worked up to see him again. I couldn't wait to feel his hands on my body, and he would tell me how he was dreaming of the day he would feel my hands on his cock or how his cock longed to be inside me. We talked about how he longed to cum inside me as well as all over me.

He caused my body to shake from states away. How was this possible? How could a man cause such physical and mental changes from so far away? The longing my mind and body had for him was uncontrollable and even if I could control it, I had no intention of doing so.

I still used Kane for sex. I know I know, it's terrible to say, but my feelings for him were never going to be anything more. Not like our Husband. He lit a fire in me not even words could describe. Our phone calls had become FaceTime calls where I could see his hand on his cock as he was stroking it. What was I supposed to do?

SISTER WIFE IS HOME

Of course, she had to make a dramatic entrance. Everything about her seemed to have a dramatic beginning and ending. Why she felt she had to always have eyes on her I couldn't figure out. At this point I figured we would all just accept it and move on but in the back of my mind I wondered if she had some sort of disorder or if her childhood was that fucked up or maybe it was both.

While she was in my home state we hung out and talked about all the typical things girls talk about. All the things except what I had been up to with our Husband. I didn't want to tell her. She was so happy to be back and hanging out with me. Of course, there was shopping and eating and sightseeing but zero talk about all our phone sex.

Eventually the day came when she had to head south to her new duty station and join our Husband. I liked having her here because she made me feel closer to him, but I knew she had to go. I also knew she would be with him. A little bit of jealousy crept up. The words of the third wife creeped up in my thoughts about how my sister wife didn't match with our Husband and how she was just not deserving of him. How she trapped him by getting pregnant on purpose so he would feel like he had to stay.

I continued thinking about what the third wife had said about our Husband and my sister wife. Do they have anything in common? What do they see in each other? I had spent enough time with them, and I began to question what the dynamics of the two of them were. He was so laid back and she was uptight. He liked quality time together and she seemed to care about how they looked in front of others.

While my mind was turning all the thoughts of them together, sister wife and I had agreed we would all meet at the Southern home during Christmas, and I would ask Jade and Karma if they wanted to join. A plan was set in motion, I was going to see him soon.

CHRISTMAS AND PLANNING A MOVE

Our Husband knew I loved the beach and the Mountains. It really didn't surprise me when I got the call about the new purchase right on top of a mountain out West. I was excited to hear about it and couldn't wait to go out and see it.

My sisters and I went south for the Christmas break to spend it with my sister wife and our Husband. We all spent time on the internet looking for used furniture to put in the new place and talked about what the inside would like after it was decorated. I ended up finding a great deal on some furniture in my home state and had it brought to my house until they were ready to pick it up.

Our Husband and I took walks every day down to the water or over to get the mail. What was really happening was a serious game of "how much can I kiss you and how much of your body can I touch without cuming in my pants."

We couldn't keep our hands off each other. We were hiding in the trees, the dark sandy beach, even over by the neighborhood pool because he knew the cameras were broken. I felt like a kid hiding a bad habit I knew was wrong, but he was so persistent, and I was so weak.

Returning home was miserable. I missed my sister wife and our Husband. I knew they missed me because my phone was blowing up with texts and calls.

Some of the texts were about random things. Others were from our Husband, sweet and a bit dirty, and talked about our kisses on the beach. He talked about how he couldn't wait to see me again, how he couldn't wait to touch me again and how he longed to feel every inch of my skin.

One of the calls from my sister wife was to ask if I would like to help move all the items into the new place out West. I was excited about the invitation but couldn't figure out how I would get back home. She assured me she would handle the returning flight and begged for me to go. She giggled while she talked about the fun, we would have but my mind drifted off to our Husband and the thoughts of him touching my skin.

I gave in and made all the arrangements I needed to make for my kids and the plan to help them move was a go.

Later, our Husband called to talk about the trip and what his plans were with my sister wife. I feel like his wording was a bit different from our previous conversations, but I listened closely to what he had to say. He was telling me how he was going to convince our wife to allow me into the bedroom. I kind of laughed a little and told him there was no way she would allow this. Who in their right mind would allow another woman into her marital bedroom?

The next thing he said made me really think she had put him up to it. He said, "She would do anything she thought you wanted her to do."

"It's almost as if she wanted you to tell her what to do."

As our conversation continued, our Husband talked about the trip and how it was going to be broken up into days of travel and days unpacking.

He continued to go back to what his plans were in the bedroom. He made it very clear before we reached our destination, he was going to fuck me without our wife. He talked about wanting to savor my body and not share with her the first time. I wasn't sure what to say but I could feel my body begin to warm in places. I was going to need a release soon.

41

MOVING DAY

I was picked up at my house early one morning. We loaded what items I had purchased for the new place into the trailer our Husband had rented. The trailer was connected to the RV van he had purchased while our wife was deployed. When my bag was loaded into the back of the van I climbed into the front seat. I always had to sit in the front seat because I would get car sick. Our wife had no issues with taking the back seat. It was weird for me, but I would gladly sit next to our Husband.

I looked at our Husband and he smiled. It was like we had a secret but did we really? Had they already talked about what they both wanted from me? I just smiled and turned on some music, trying to enjoy the ride.

While looking out the window, I thought about last Christmas and how our Husband would caress my skin every time he thought no one would see. How his breath felt on my neck when he was able to get close enough. Thoughts of him taking my whole body ran through my mind as I drifted off in and out of sleep.

After hours of driving, our Husband began to talk about where we were stopping for the night. He had made a reservation at a campground for us to stop and sleep. We were in a van/RV that also had a bed, bathroom and a tiny kitchen. Tiny little living space but the king size bed was what our Husband was most interested in that night.

We finally stopped and got the van all hooked up for the

night. The campground had a nice bathroom/shower facility, and it was a fairly quiet campground. All three of us snuggled in for the night. It wasn't weird for me to sleep in the same bed with them. My sister wife was in the middle and she and I had slept in the same bed before, so it was nothing new for me.

I slept so well that first night. I'm not sure if it was being on the road all day or if I was just exhausted from my mind being on overdrive. I mean, how could anyone not be exhausted from thinking about our Husband all day and the anticipation of having sex with him?

It was waking up the next morning that was a bit of a surprise. It was our Husband's hand that woke me. It was warm and soft against my skin. I was laying there as if I were sleeping, he slid his hand down into my panties and had inserted his finger into my now wet pussy.

My body stiffened, and I let out a gasp. I wasn't sure if it was from panic or excitement. I instantly began looking for my sister wife, scared she was there seeing what he was doing to me. He assured me she wasn't inside the van and that she had left to take a shower.

He began to kiss my neck and rub my breasts. My body lit up like a fire soaked in gasoline. My whole body was tingling, and my head was spinning. His warm breath was on my face, and I could feel the heat coming off his hard cock as it touched my bare leg. I was definitely not resisting, and neither was my body.

He was going to fuck me. He told me before he was going to fuck me before my sister wife was allowed to have a taste and he was about to follow through with it. I was laying there thinking about his words until he slid his warm cock across the outside of my pussy, and I lost all ability to think rationally. I wanted him just as much as he wanted me.

He then migrated his hard, warm cock into my welcoming, wet pussy. As he began to move his cock, I couldn't help but shove my pelvis into him needing more. With every thrust, my body would crash into his with a craving I have not felt in years. Our bodies were voltaic next to one another. Was I really feeling so many breathtaking emotions? How can one man cause so much electricity?

While we were fucking, I opened my eyes to look into his. Instead, I saw a reflection in the ceiling of the van. I was looking right at his bare ass. Watching him as he moved his body up and down while he fucked me was erotic. It caused my body to react in erratic and involuntary ways. Sex was more than physical for me but seeing him in such a vulnerable way caused so many emotions.

Just as my body and my mind were becoming submerged into him, he let out a moan. His body stiffened while he slammed his cock so hard into me and his face reddened. He was cuming and it was apparently an exceptional one. He was holding his breath as he thrusted his dick in me again several more times. When he finished his body went limp, he laid his entire weight on me and let out a breath with such fulfillment.

It was amazing to feel his skin on mine and to feel him inside me. To finally know all of him and not just what he was allowed to show me in public. At this point my mind was fulfilled but my body was discontented. He came before my body was ready, but I somehow was OK with this feeling of physical discontentment. First times are always a bit different, but I didn't expect to feel satisfied and dissatisfied all at the same time.

I finally was able to catch my breath and I began to collect my personal items for a shower. Our Husband was telling me how incredible it was making love to me. He continued by saying he had never had a fuck so involved or satisfying in his entire life. Hearing that made my lack of orgasm and satisfaction not such a let-down.

Walking into the shower house my mind drifted to what had just happened in the van. Steam came rolling out of the shower stall where my sister wife was showering. The mirrors by the sink fogged up, I smiled at her and wondered if she knew. Could she see the guilt and the pleasure on my face? I could only imagine what my face was saying that my mouth wasn't.

She asked if I slept well and told me the showers were hot and the pressure was good. Like nothing happened, like there was zero guilt on my face. She walked over to the door of the shower house and with a giggle, told me to enjoy my shower. Wait, was this all her idea? Is this why she decided to shower so early?

So many questions ran through my mind as I was showering. She had to know what happened. Was our Husband telling her all about it while I was in the shower?

She had to know what happened whether it was her idea or our Husband's. Was he telling her all about it while I showered? Was my sister wife listening to all the details of our love making? Did she know?

I had several hours in the van with both my sister wife and our Husband before we arrived at the new place. I again put on some music, looked at the scenery out the window and let my mind spin in circles.

ARRIVAL AT THE NEW PLACE

When we pulled into the parking space, it was snowing. We were high enough in elevation that the snow was continuing to fall. I loved snow, it had an aphrodisiac effect on me, and I felt like I couldn't hide or keep it under control. Our Husband knew this and used this secret information to his advantage.

The looks and glances he would give me from across the room were beginning to make me weak. I blamed the thin air of the mountains but we both knew it was from the flashes of our morning coitus. The pats on my ass and the casual touching from our Husband were definitely not helping when it came to keeping me focused on the move.

We spent most of the day unloading the trailer. Moving all the big furniture was a bit harder in high elevations because of the thinner air. I also used that excuse when I would excuse myself for a break. With the three of us, we were able to finish moving all the furniture and household supplies by early evening.

My sister wife began fixing dinner while I made the bed in the bedroom and pulled the sofa bed out for myself. I had a little time before dinner, so I decided to shower. I did all I could to think about other things, but my mind kept going back to the start of my day. The way our Husband woke me, the gentle touches, the way he caressed my skin. Before I realized it, I found myself breathing heavily and wanting more. Even though I was left unsatisfied I just needed more.

When I came out of the bathroom, dinner was still not done

so I decided to unpack my things. I could feel his eyes on me as I emptied my bag and laid my clothes out for the next day. It was almost intoxicating, and I again started to breathe a little heavier than normal. I blamed it on the mountain air when sister wife asked me if I was OK.

I had to stop and occupy my mind with something else so I walked into the kitchen to see if there was anything I could help with as far as dinner or unpacking. Sister wife told me to just relax until dinner was ready. I walked over and sat on the sofa bed and waited for dinner.

Dinner was OK. We had some sort of ground meat on a bun and a salad. Sister wasn't much of a cook. I could tell by the way things tasted, very bland. I wondered if the rest of her life was just as bland. Is this why I was here? To spice things up between them? To make their lives "spicier"?

I did dinner dishes while sister took a shower. Our Husband seemed to be busy unpacking his things and moving the bedroom furniture to where he liked it. He also organized the closet with the extra cleaning items we were leaving for the use of the possible renters.

When sister finished her shower, she and I unpacked the rest of the kitchen items while our Husband showered. Sister didn't talk about anything serious or about anything that happened that morning. Before we all knew it, it was late and time for bed. We had unpacking to finish and some exploring of the area the next day.

We all said good night and headed to our separate beds. When my sister wife said goodnight, there was a smile on her face I hadn't seen before. I again wondered if she was the one who orchestrated this entire scenario.

I laid on the couch sofa for about fifteen minutes replaying the smile she had on her face before I started to doze off. Just as I was falling asleep, I felt a hand on my arm. It was our Husband. He motioned for me to get out of bed.

He pulled my hand towards him and lifted me out of bed. My heart felt like it was beating out of my chest and so fast there was no way my breathing could keep up. My body started shaking. His hand was so soft and his touch so gentle.

I stood up and looked him in the eyes, he said, "She would like to talk to you in the bedroom." He then led me to the door.

When I looked in, my sister wife was covered with a sheet. I could tell she was naked. It was the way she was holding the sheet over her breast that gave it away. With a wave of her hand, she motioned for me to come lay beside her. I looked at our Husband and his face was lit with anticipation. The same smile I saw early that morning was the one I was looking at. He motioned his hand towards the bed.

What am I doing? What have I gotten myself into? Have they done this before? What are they expecting from me? How is this done? What am I supposed to do? So many questions were spinning around in my head and I couldn't stop them or answer them.

He took my hand, put his other hand on the small of my back and led me to the bed where she was laying. My sister wife grabbed my other hand when I reached the bedside. Gently pulling me to the bed, she smiled at me and took a deep breath.

Before I was able to grasp what hit me, I could feel her tongue in my mouth and his hands pressed against my clitoris. Her mouth left mine, she ran her tongue down my neck and to my nipples. I let out a moan so low but loud I barely heard the moan sister let out while she wrapped her tongue around my nipple. Her breathing began to match mine which caused me to slip into a state of mind I had never experienced.

Our Husband slid his cock into me slowly and gently while our wife watched. She liked it? She wanted to see him fuck someone else? Has she watched this before? Am I not the first one for them? Has he fucked someone else in front of sister before? Am I not her first sister wife? I snapped out of it when she bit my nipple and I let out a small cry.

Sister moaned with pleasure knowing I felt her teeth as she bit me. I went back to my thoughts once she released my nipple from her teeth. She liked it! She liked watching him fuck me while she aroused my nipples and made them hard. She began to rub my inner thigh, trying to feel my slit as his cock would slam into me. With her other hand, she began to rub her own pussy with the motion of our Husband and I fucking.

She was getting aroused by this. She liked it. She approved seeing us together, naked, sweaty and completely engrossed with each other. I could also see by the look on her face sister had a desire to watch what we were doing and be involved.

As we were fucking, she moved her head closer to his cock. I was trying to imagine how she was going to put his dick in her mouth. Her face got closer and closer to his cock, and I could feel her warm breath on my stomach. She was going for his swollen dick. Sister took in a deep breath and let out what sounded like a sigh and then I felt her tongue on my clit. It wasn't him she wanted, it was me. She wanted to taste me, to lick me, to please me.

The harder she rubbed my clit with her wet tongue, the harder our Husband fucked me. I couldn't stop my body from thrusting my pussy into his cock and her tongue. I was about to cum all over them. I couldn't stop, everything was out of control. I was out of control.

It hit me like I was running into a waterfall in the middle of the desert. The shock, intensity, the breathtaking deafening orgasm was beyond anything I had ever felt in my life. I couldn't breathe and as much as I wanted to thrust myself into his cock, I grabbed the back off my wife's head and slammed it into my clit. The rest of the orgasm is a blur of something I can't even describe.

With a ringing in my ear, I slowly opened my eyes and attempted to relax my body. My breathing was rapid, my body covered in sweat and the smell of sex. He smiled at me with a smile of a man who just conquered the implausible. He looked at me with so much desire and asked me if there was anything else, I needed from either of them. I could only shake my head no. My entire body was spent. My wife then shoved her index finger and middle finger into my dripping wet pussy. When she pulled them out, she licked one and our Husband licked the other. Both fixating on my eyes, neither of them breaking the intense eye contact.

He then grabbed our wife and fucked her until he came. It was mostly uneventful aside a few moans and her need to touch my breast while he was fucking her. Did she always just lay there like a dead fish? Did she just fake her orgasm? Did she get anything from fucking him at all?

Lost in thought, I didn't feel our Husband get out of bed. He reached for my hand and pulled me towards the edge of the bed. My eyes met his and I could see the satisfaction in his eyes. I too was satisfied, and I hoped he could see how satisfied I felt. We all three then headed for the shower, covered in cum, saliva and sweat.

Standing in the shower with the water falling over my face, our wife stood behind me and rubbed my back. She washed my hair and helped our Husband wash my body. She was acting as if I was some type of predominant and it was her place to clean me before we went to bed.

She called me ma'am and asked me if there was anything else she could do for me in the shower. I should have seen this as a "red flag" but I was so focused on our Husband to see past (as my father always said) "the end of my nose."

When our shower ended, they led me back to the bedroom and asked if I would sleep there, with them. I did, but not well. The bed was small, we were crowded, and my mind was spinning out of control. I couldn't stop thinking about the chain of events, the way our Husband looked at me and the way he continued to touch me throughout the night.

THE DAY AFTER

When morning came, our Husband was up and out of bed first. He was in the living area waiting for his wives to get out of bed. He was a morning person and enjoyed watching as the world woke up around him.

I woke up to my sister wife looking at me as she laid beside me. She smiled as I looked at her and I wasn't sure what to think. She appeared to be happy or at least content with herself and me. When she decided to get up, she told me to rest, and she would make coffee. Was she thinking about last night? Was she as delighted as she was portraying herself to be?

It was kind of a weird day for me. My sister wife couldn't keep her hands off me. Every chance she had, she would brush up against me or touch my ass as I would walk by her. She made it a point to work on things that were close to me. The condo was coming along, and sister's teasing never stopped.

Our Husband watched her playful touching, and it was obvious he wanted to do more than touch me. The place was small so brushing his crotch up against me so I could feel his swollen dick became a game for him. He knew what he was doing, he knew the more he brushed up against me the harder it was for me to focus on anything.

My body was tingling from head to toe, and I could feel my crotch getting wetter and wetter. There was only so much of this I could handle. I wasn't the only one having issues with focusing on putting the place together. One of us was going to break and it was going to happen soon.

Just as the thought ran through my mind, sister grabbed my breasts and shoved her tongue in my mouth with such force I may have bit her. He then came up behind me and grabbed me by my inner thigh. I grabbed her ponytail and with one pull I dragged my sister wife into the bedroom. Our Husband didn't pause to think as he shoved both of us down onto the bed.

"Who wants my dick first and where do you want it?" Before sister wife had time to say anything, I demanded she get up and stick it in her mouth. Without any hesitation, she grabbed his dick and shoved it in her mouth. She pushed her head forward then backward and our Husband put his hand on the back of her head to help her with her rhythm.

A couple of minutes went by, and she paused. She looked at me and asked, "Is this what you want, ma'am?"

"Is there something else I could do to please you?"

What was this? Was she looking for me to tell her what to do and how to do it? Ma'am? Did she just say that? She needed my approval and wanted to please me? I had to test this thought process. I needed more information of what she was pushing my role to be.

I demanded she stop sucking on his dick and to start licking my clit. She's a woman and well, our bodies are all very similar, so her tongue was arousing. Also, I have never had a woman like that before. I felt the need to watch her as I pressed my clit into her mouth. She moaned with what I thought was pleasure and when I looked at her, she seemed to be enjoying herself.

I pulled her hair to pull her mouth off me. The look on her face was nothing but happiness. I told her to wet our Husband's rock-hard cock with her dripping mouth. I then told her to put into my wanting pussy so he could fuck me.

She slid her hand to his cock slowly while watching my face. While she was inserting it, she brushed her fingers across my pussy and then up to her mouth. She likes the way I taste. From the looks of it, she couldn't get enough of me.

Fucking him was not just exciting but fulfilling this time. It was like he was waiting for me to cum before he did. Was he putting me first? Did he know he hadn't made me cum before? I hope not. Disappointing him was the last thing I wanted to do and knowing this would do just that.

When we were finished, we all got up and dressed. They both went about the rest of the day like it was a normal thing. It was like this was normal for them. The last hour was something I never thought would happen. Both were acting as if this was something normal and I wasn't sure how to act. I was almost certain this was planned, I was planned.

My head spinning, my pussy still throbbing from him slamming into it with his cock, I was still trying to make sense of everything that had happened. This was not normal for me, and I wasn't sure how to act. I was trying to act normal like they were but I'm sure my face was saying what my mouth wasn't.

I sat on the couch and reached for my phone when I saw it light up. I had gotten a new email alert and looking at my email sent me into a spiral. How could my sister wife do this to me without asking? It was intentional, and she knew what she was doing.

SHE WENT BEHIND MY BACK

I read an email from the gym in the Southern state where my sister wife was telling me my daughter should go. They were welcoming my daughter to their gym and talked about how excited they were to have her on their team.

I remember seeing a contract from my sister wife. She had printed it out and given it to me. She was begging me to move into the spare room with my daughter. I told her I wasn't sure, so she filled it out and signed my name to it. I was now in a legal contract with the gym.

When I talked to my sister wife, she told me it wasn't until August, so I had the summer to get ready if I wanted. I asked her how the gym even accepted her? The website for the gym made it clear there were specific dates for tryouts for the team and if you couldn't make it, to send a video of very specific skills for them to evaluate. I hadn't done either of those things.

Sister wife reminded me of all the times we had visited for holidays, and she went to the gym as a visitor for workout days. They already knew my daughter and they already loved her. She was in and part of the team.

My sister wife let me know she would have the room ready for me by the time I was packed and ready to move. She told me it was best for everyone as she grinned. She looked very pleased with herself, her face beaming with a mixture of happiness and pleasure.

She began to remind me about Kane and how he calls me

names daily. She began to list the names he called me and how he compared me to his ex. She kept telling me about how he would demand things and tell me I was useless.

Sister continued about how our kids were friends and with me in the same house, it would make their military life easier. I would be the backup plan for the girls when the military had them doing other things or when they needed to see the doctor and they couldn't get leave to take them.

By the time she was finished with her list of all the things they needed me for other than sexual pleasure and reminded me about the contract I knew I was moving.

I decided to keep the moving part to myself, with the exception of Raven, and the lawyer I needed to draw up the documents necessary to take her with me.

ONE LAST VISIT

I planned a trip down to see them with my actual sisters before the move. Karma and Jade loved being there. It was relaxing for them, and they were able to unwind from having daily stressors. The beach was always a great place to unwind and relax.

They did mention they were a bit scared of my sister wife because of her loud, angry outburst and other behaviors she would exhibit but made it clear if I was to leave the house they were also going to go for a walk and leave. Being stuck with her alone wasn't something they wanted. I didn't blame them; I didn't like being alone with her most of the time either.

One of the first few nights we were there, Jade and Karma decided they wanted to see the sunrise the next morning. I had zero desire to get out of bed to walk down to the beach to watch the sun come up. Not only had I been drinking that night but I was too tired to move.

I let them both know I was still too tired when they got up and tried to drag me out of bed. Or so I thought. Not even three minutes after they left, our Husband came into my room. His cock was clearly hard and wanting a morning fuck. He looked at me with his seductive eyes as he locked the bedroom door.

He crawled into my bed and removed my panties before I realized what was happening. He wasted no time slipping his dick into my pussy. He began to fuck me with such force it instantly woke all my senses. I was no longer tired. I was awake and my entire body was shivering with excitement.

His excitement was over the top. It showed when he lasted only a few minutes. He came so quickly my body had no time to respond. Fucked and unsatisfied again. If this was going to continue, I was going to have to find a way other than self-gratification. I needed to figure out how his body worked so I could sink mine with his. Otherwise, this was never going to work.

The following day was going to be our last until big the move that no one saw coming. We all spent time together outside in the yard and at the beach. It was like I was the only one who had a care in the world.

My worries started to diminish watching our Husband walk down to the water. Watching him lower himself in the water and pop back up all wet was something you would imagine seeing in a movie. I wanted to look at Karma and Jade and tell them everything. I had to stop myself. No one could know at this point, so I put it out of my head.

That evening when my sister wife was fixing dinner, my sisters were packing, and our Husband and I decided to go for a walk. Walks with our Husband usually turned into interesting adventures. Sometimes they were just walks where we would talk about life and things we enjoy. Other times it turned into enjoying each other.

He couldn't keep his hands off me. If we were behind a house, tree or construction dumpster he was all over me. We walked down to get the mail and he led me into the pool area. We both knew the cameras didn't work but we were still in an open area running the risk of being seen. This made me nervous but also very excited.

He grabbed my hand and punched in the number to the club house bathroom entrance keypad and the lock released the door.

He tried the first door, and it was locked. He found the equipment door unlocked and pushed me in, locking the door behind him. Throwing me on the floor on top of an inflatable swim mat he threw my shirt up over my head, ripping it in the process. I didn't care. I could feel his breath on my skin, it was hot, sending shivers down my spine. I took his pants off as he was kissing every piece of bare skin he could find.

We are about to fuck in the club house. He didn't care where we were or who could hear us. He looked me right in my eyes as he shoved his dick into me. He began to tell me how great of a fuck I was and how I made his dick constantly hard. While he continued to fuck me, I asked if he liked cuming inside me.

We both talked the entire time we were fucking. Talking about how hot it was and how we couldn't get enough of each other. He loved it when I would beg for him to cum for me. The more I begged the harder he fucked me. When he came, he looked right into my eyes and asked me if this was what I wanted. Yes, yes it was!

When we were finished and we left the club house, we talked all the way back to the house. He said our wife was much happier with me in the house and seemed even more sexually satisfied when I was a part of their interaction. He seemed happy, and his smile was all I needed to feel content with our situation.

I looked at him and told him not to allow me to fall in love with him if this wasn't a permanent thing. My heart couldn't handle another heartbreak and he knew this. I also told him living there was expensive, and I couldn't afford to do that on my own. He laughed and said he had enough money to support me and my daughter and not to worry. He then looked at me and told me, not only did he love me, but he was also in love with me.

Returning to the house he repeated my concerns to my sister

wife. She pulled me to the side and told me I would never have to worry about anything ever again. She was going to take care of me and was excited about having me in the house full time. She kissed my cheek and told me she loved me and was in love with me and couldn't imagine going through life without me.

She made me feel so loved and I was told love can get you through anything, so I closed my eyes and jumped fearlessly without a second thought.

PACKING UP AND PREPARING TO LEAVE

When we returned to my home state, I began packing my things and so did my daughter. All the paperwork was in order and all I needed to do was load the car and go.

Saying I was nervous and excited at the same time would be an understatement. How could I be so happy, scared and excited all at the same time? It's him, our Husband, he brings feelings out of me I thought were lost forever.

I explained to Kane I was needed there to help with their kids while they worked and deployed. It was like talking to the wall and expecting it to understand the words.

I mean, it was the truth, it just wasn't the entire truth. I left out the parts where I was having sex with our Husband and my sister wife. I also left out the part where my sister wife was making it to where I would be dependent on her and our Husband.

As I was trying to explain to Kane I would be back and forth my phone started buzzing. It was my sister wife. She was sending links to short stories she wanted me to read before my return. Kane was getting angrier by the second.

I had planned on leaving in a week or so but with his anger building, I decided leaving sooner was going to be necessary. Kane was acting aggressive, and our Husband was beginning to act like I was taking too long.

I went to bed early that night and did some reading my sister wife sent before falling asleep. I opened the link she had sent and was a bit taken back. It was a short story about a man who

61

dominated over his woman.

This story was full of dominating activities and punishments for not listening to the directions given to the submissive. He shamed her and punished her for the slightest bit of obstinance. What was she saying to me? What was she wanting from me?

Again, I should have looked at the big picture before I agreed but my need for kindness and love had been promised to be met if I moved and my daughter's need for a gym of this nature would also be met. I had to go.

I started drifting off to sleep while I was reading, and my phone started buzzing. It was sister wife, she sent me a list.

THE LIST

The day before we were to leave, my sister wife sent me a link. She told me it was some ideas she wanted me to look at on punishments she wanted me to consider when she was bad. I was confused for a minute, but then realized she wanted to be my Submissive (Sub).

I have a very dominant personality and I'm very forward with what I want or how I feel things should go. Sister wife could see that side of me existed and she wanted it. She apparently wanted the entire dominatrix I was holding inside me to come out.

She was looking for spankings and not soft ones either. She wanted to be tied up and whipped until she bled. She wanted marks, battle wounds. She wanted to be able to look at them for days. She wanted to savor them and remember what had occurred during punishments. There were several punishments involving ice, candle wax and gagging.

There was another list on how to deny her pleasure, sleep and sometimes basic needs like water and food. There were time out tactics, remote control vibrators and shock clamps.

Other lists were punishments using items to force in her ass and others to force her to use her ass muscles to hold the items inside her.

She typed out a list for me to think about for her punishments. She also sent me a list of things she did where she felt she deserved punishment.

What was happening? Did she really want me to hit her with a belt? Did she want to see bruises for days? She wanted to bleed from me hitting her with whips and riding crops? The more I thought about it the more confused I became but I was not going to let this stop me from moving.

I had to move. Moving was what was best for me and for Raven. I had already done things out of my character for our Husband so what were a few more things?

I continued to go through the links of lists she sent me. Wondering if our Husband had any idea this is what she had in store for me. Had he lured me in for this purpose? Was he wanting to watch me do this to her? Was this something she had asked him for, and he couldn't perform? Did she ask him to bring me in to take care of what he was not capable of doing?

ARRIVAL DAY

When we left home Kane had left early for work. He was not in the mood to talk to me, nor did he want to say goodbye. He was angry as always and wanted nothing to do with me. The voice of sister wife in my head telling me Kane acted this way because he never loved me.

The drive was long, but I was too excited to stop and rest. I wanted to get there and begin this new journey with my new family. I knew their kids were not happy about the move and voiced their anger about having a "babysitter" in the house. My sister wife assured me it would be OK and not to worry.

I played all the ways things could go right or wrong in my head on the drive. So many ways it could go right but the ways it could go wrong didn't matter at this point. I had our Husband and Raven. All I would ever need while staying with my new family.

When we pulled into the driveway, my spouses came out the front door. They looked so happy. I got all kinds of hugs and seeing their happiness made me feel a bit more at ease.

Walking into the house, both Eve and Trista stomped up the stairs and slammed their bedroom doors. They were not happy. I would have thought Trista, the middle daughter, would have been a bit more excited due to being friends with Raven. I guess I should have taken it a bit more seriously than I did. They showed their disdain for Raven and I but I had no idea what they had in store for us. Raven and I just went to the room they had ready for us and turned in for the night.

END OF SUMMER

We had moved towards the end of summer. School was going to start soon, and my sister wife decided we were going to homeschool them because of all the training hours at the gym. I agreed it was a good idea and began to research ways to keep the girls on track.

This time of the year is always so busy with school and gym. Getting up early to work on school and staying up late because of training at the gym. Raven and Trista had longer hours than Eve. They were far more advanced and with being a higher level there are more hours and days of training.

That is when life decided to throw a wrench into our lives. Our Husband was getting deployed, and my sister wife was having surgery that would keep her off her feet for weeks literally. Surgery on her foot and our Husband having to go halfway around the world. How was I going to cope with it all?

Suddenly, I had a lot of responsibility on top of keeping everyone happy. Our Husband was doing what he could to stay light-hearted. He loved playing the game of "grab ass." I didn't mind, it kept my mind off him leaving and being left with sister wife, Trista and Eve. I did what I could to stay light-hearted, but I was almost certain our Husband could see right through me.

My end of summer wasn't turning out like I wanted. He was leaving, the girls were shitty to Raven and myself. Sister wife blamed everyone for everything but herself. Nothing was ever her fault.

TRIP TO THE SPRINGS

Our Husband decided we were going to take one last trip before he was sent to the great big sandbox on the other side of the planet. He talked with me and with sister wife about what he would like to do and wanted to know what our opinions were. I was ready to do whatever he wanted just to spend a little more time with him before he left.

It was decided, we were going to a semi-local place that had a natural spring. The water was cold, but it was so hot outside it was going to feel great.

The big van was loaded with all the items we needed for camping and swimming. Our Husband then went and picked up a small pull behind camper they also owned for all the girls to sleep in.

When the girls found out the adults were going to be in the big van, they were not pleased. Our Husband didn't seem to care how they felt about it and went about his preparations. Sister wife decided it was time to pick a fight with Eve. We could never go anywhere without sister causing an issue with someone.

I decided to skip the drama and load my things in the van. Raven also loaded her things, and we sat on the front porch to wait for the temper tantrums to stop.

Once we were on the road, sister wife kept to herself with her face in her phone. She played games until we reached the springs. I was thankful she was quiet. It made the ride over so much more enjoyable. It left me imagining what this extended weekend trip was going to be like.

First day was quiet. The girls went to the springs to swim while the adults set up camp. Of course, our Husband packed all the wrong things and not enough of what he did pack, and nothing was where it was supposed to be. If he stepped right, sister wife was yelling because he should have gone left.

I watched him as sister wife yelled and degraded him. Our poor Husband was taking a mental beating. I think he would have felt better had she just slapped him in the face. Sister's words stung and the hurt I could see, hurt me just as much. I had to intervene.

I told sister wife to take a minute and our Husband to go check on the girls. I would help sister finish setting up the camp if our Husband could just make sure the girls were OK. Off he went without a second for anyone to change their mind.

Camp was set, dinner was ready, and things were calm. When our Husband came back with the girls, he looked so much better than what he did when he left. This made me happy. I was ready for dinner to be over, and for everyone to go to bed. I wanted to snuggle up next to him and listen to his heartbeat while he slept.

Morning came fast. I didn't want to get up. Staying in his arms with sister on the other side was right where I wanted to be. Morning meant it had to end and we all had to get up.

The girls were wired for play. Right after breakfast, they were ready for swimming and sun. Raven and I sat on the bank of the spring for a bit talking about sister wife and her explosion the day before. I think we both were hoping it was just a rare occurrence. I told Raven not to worry and to go swimming with the rest of them.

That afternoon, after lunch, I went into the beg van to use

the bathroom. Sister wife followed me in, and our Husband was right behind her. When I came out of the bathroom, they were both on the bed. Our Husband reached up and grabbed my hand and pulled me towards the bed.

I was nervous because all the girls were right outside the van. When he kissed me, I couldn't help but let go and follow his pull into the bed. His hands were so soft, his breathing on my skin intoxicating.

He then turned to sister wife and kissed her. It didn't seem to have the passion I had felt. I quietly asked if all the doors were locked, and sister assured me she locked the doors when she came in. Our Husband looked at me and asked if I wanted to be fucked first. Just as sister was reaching over to touch me breast, Eve flung the back door of the van open. Sister yelled at her and tried to grab the handle. Because they were making such a scene, I was able to cover myself and hope no one saw me laying there. Sister kept yelling at Eve until Eve slammed the door.

I don't blame her for opening the door. The van was rocking from the hard fucking our Husband was giving us and the girls knew all three of us were in the van. I waited to leave the van for several minutes after my loves left. None of the girls said anything for hours about the incident. Even though they weren't talking I could clearly see what they wanted to say by the looks on their faces.

Raven later pulled me to the side and asked what was going on in the van while it was rocking. I had to lie. I couldn't upset her or the other girls before their dad left for deployment. I looked at Raven and told her I had gone in to go to the bathroom. Next thing I knew the van was rocking and I was stuck in the bathroom until it was over. Raven laughed and asked if I was going to have nightmares later. I hated lying to her, it hurt my heart to lie to her.

I just couldn't find the words to tell her the truth.

The next morning it was time to pack up the camp and go home. As usual, sister was barking orders and then screaming because none of us could do what she wanted the right way. Sister's attitude made for a long ride home. I'm not sure why I thought she would stop once we were all in the van.

I was so happy when this trip was over. Sister wife and Eve fought for the next couple of days. It was the kind of fighting that made Raven and I walk away like we didn't know who they were. I felt terrible for our Husband but those two were being crazy. I was starting to wonder if they could be anything but crazy.

Returning to the house was sad. This meant our Husband was leaving very soon and I was going alone with sister who seemed to want to torment Eve. Eve who seemed to want to scream, yell, and hit anyone who got in her way. Trista who talked nice to your face but was a complete bitch behind your back (we found out later) and gave a new meaning to "two faced." I wasn't sure I was going to make it.

...

The day came for him to leave, and I had a lot of difficulty keeping myself together. I was so thankful for the sweet love making the night before and the promise of his return. He was so kind, and I was determined to help sister control herself and her temper before he returned because he deserved to be treated with just as much care as he was giving.

I spent a lot of time in my room after he left that day. He assured me it would go fast, and he would be back in my arms soon. I held onto that so hard, reminding myself this chaos was temporary.

WHILE HE WAS DEPLOYED

Things were kind of crazy at the house daily. My sister wife fought with Eve every single day. There were things broken in the house and they beat the crap out of each other. It was almost like sister wanted to fight with Eve even if there was nothing to fight about. It was chaos with sister all the time.

Did sister not know how to act like a normal person? Watching her with her girls, I was scared she would take it too far and seriously hurt one of them. There were days I would watch her with Eve and see the transition of her mood and personality. It was like sister was a different person and that person wanted Eve to suffer.

It was a usual occurrence for me to punish her after she argued with her kids. They would leave to go to the gym, and she would go into the bathroom and braid her hair. She would then undress down to nothing and lay face down on the bed with a wedge type pillow under her midsection. She would wait there until I came into the bedroom.

The severity of her punishments would at times depend on my mood. On days I lost patience, I would immediately go into the bedroom just to get it over with. Other times I would wait sometimes over an hour just to punish her even more. Mostly because of what she was looking for in punishment, I had to build up the courage to give her.

She begged to be beaten with belts. She wanted marks she could see for days. If she was bleeding, she enjoyed it even more.

The tighter I tied her up the more she seemed to enjoy the beatings. She loved Trista counting the swats, but she really liked it when no one was home, and I could make her scream. Shoving butt plugs in her ass and ben-wa balls in her pussy and beating her at the same time was a lot for me.

Why did she feel like she needed to be beaten so bad? Why did she crave harder and harder spankings? I knew she was getting serious with the beatings when she came home with a cane. Now she wanted me to hit her with a wooden cane the way I did with the belt, and I was a bit scared. Did she know what kind of damage a cane could do to a person? I could scar her. Did she want scars? Could I live with myself if I did scar her? Did our Husband know she wanted this type of treatment? Did he beat her?

As I hit her, she would let out a scream she attempted to mask with a pillow. Screaming was not allowed during punishments and sister knew this. The scream was not only a scream of pain but also had a hint of pleasure mixed in. I knew the cane had to hurt. When I saw the blood on her ass from the mark the cane left, she shifted and turned to look at me.

She wasn't allowed to move or make noise during punishment time and if she did, I added more swats. (One of sister's rules.) She knew this and sometimes I think she moved and screamed on purpose.

Now that she had shifted and was looking at me, I swung the cane again. I was attempting to hit the same spot that was bleeding to make it hurt even more. I was successful. Sister screamed and begged for mercy, but I didn't stop. She wanted pain and I gave it to her. I wish I could have told her then, the physical pain she was feeling was killing me on the inside. I hated hurting her, but she demanded it. She used what I needed for myself and Raven as incentive to do as she asked. I made sure there were marks and blood. I would do whatever I had to, to make sure Raven had everything she needed and wanted.

Would I be able to keep this up the entire time our Husband was gone? I tried to be strong. When our Husband would call, I would cry a lot and beg him to find a reason to come home. I needed him home. I wanted to go home. Not the home I was living in but the one I left. I felt so alone even in a house full of people.

Why would our Husband leave me in such a mess? Why would he leave me with sister, knowing I hate violence? Not only did she want me to be violent to her but she was naturally violent towards Eve. Why would he leave me in Hell?

While talking to him I told him I wanted to go home. I was not able to be a part of the family like he wanted. I couldn't make sister happy and keep her from mentally killing the girls. Nothing was making sister happy, and I was over killing myself trying.

TILL DEATH DO US PART

At one point, my sister wife decided we were going to have an unofficial, official wedding ceremony so we could be married. She made jokes that it wasn't an elevator, but the kids were still in attendance.

One of her girls, Eve, officiated and Trista was a flower girl. Raven was Maid of Honor and the DJ for the wedding music. We had flowers, wine and she made a big deal out of it. She then called our Husband to tell him it was official, and we were all married.

While talking to him, sister was so excited about making me officially family. She was proud to be married to both of us and continued to talk about how her "spouses" were the best. She showered me with so much affection. Not just verbal affection but random pats and touching if I walked by her.

For a few days it was like she was a different person. She was happy or at least acted the part. She smiled more and I caught her being nice to Eve a couple of times. It didn't last long. It was like someone flipped a switch and suddenly, sister was back to her old habits.

It would have been nice if it would have made a difference in having any type of say of what was going on inside the house. I felt most days I was living a nightmare. I say nightmare because I had no control over anything happening inside the house. I just wanted to wake up and it all be perfect.

All the screaming and physical violence between sister and

Eve were beginning to take a toll on me. I was married to a violent man before who tried to kill us all. It started with screaming and yelling and escalated. I could see the pattern with sister and Eve. Eve had zero problems with beating the shit out of sister and sister had no issues with telling us Eve was just like that and will be in prison one day. The mental abuse didn't stop there, it extended to family outside the house as well.

I recall a day when my sister wife invited her father over for dinner. Not sure what she was thinking because he and I mixed like oil and water. Not only did he and I not get along, but sister hated her dad.

She would tell me stories about her upbringing and the way they treated each other that made sister and Eve look mild in comparison. Maybe that was part of sister's problem, her childhood. If it was so bad, why would she want to do the same thing to Eve and Trista? Was Rebecca just as bad? I didn't have time to stop and think about it, her father was coming over.

I helped prepare the meal hoping he would just eat and leave if it was ready when he got there. Unfortunately, he was the last one at the table. He was still cutting his steak and eating slower than molasses in the winter while I cleared the table.

My sister wife thought it was funny when she noticed my agitation level was rising. I immediately went into Dom mode. I opened the kitchen drawer and grabbed a wooden spoon. I pointed it to the counter where she was to bend over and place her hands. She turned to look at her dad and I looked at her with a very displeasing expression. She moved to the counter and placed her hands on the edge. I kicked the inside of her calf in a way to make her spread her legs slightly. I looked at Trista and told her I needed her to count as I swung the spoon and hit my sister wife with such force everyone but her father and myself gasped.

I didn't stop there, I continued to hit her with the spoon as Trista counted. Not one time did her father look up from his dinner plate. He continued to eat like nothing was happening. How could anyone do that? The sound of the spoon hitting her ass was loud and made a sound the neighbors could hear. Still, her father never moved from eating his dinner.

I looked at Trista who had a smile on her face as she was counting. She was also enjoying this. Literally What the Fuck? Her grin was genuine and grew as I hit her mother with the spoon. Why did Trista enjoy this so much? Did she like to see her mom in pain? Was she just as fucked up as everyone else in the family but better at hiding it?

Later that evening, my sister wife came into my room. At this point we just slept together in the same room. When she laid down, a slight wince came out. I knew she was feeling the fruits of my labor from earlier. Every move she made had to hurt.

As I was starting to fall asleep, she began to talk. She started talking about how she liked being spanked in front of the kids and how it turned her on. It made it even more erotic for her because Trista was counting. She requested I do it again as she rubbed her clit with her finger. She continued to tell me how much it aroused her as she masturbated next to me. She continued talking about how our Husband couldn't arouse her. How it was aggravating to her to always finish his job herself.

Why couldn't I have fallen asleep earlier? I just laid there as if I were sleeping. I didn't want her to know I had heard what she said. She would later use this against me and repeat her words. Did our husband know she was doing this? Did he know she was faking it the entire marriage? I had a feeling there was a lot she was hiding from our Husband, and I was thinking about how uncomfortable those thoughts were. I loved her but I loved him first and most.

WHAT HAPPENS IN VEGAS...

While our Husband was deployed, we had to take a trip to Vegas for a meet for the girls. It was one I was looking forward to for quite some time. Vegas is such a fascinating place and I love seeing all the lights. The night life was even more entertaining.

We stayed in a house on the outskirts of downtown. It was a little quieter there and since we were all homeschooling there were less distractions. It was also free because it was with a person I used to be related to.

I was told before we went by sister, we would have a guide to show us around town and to the best places to take the kids. When our guide showed up, I had no idea it would be our Husbands "brother."

He has a brother? Was he a blood brother or someone that claimed to be his brother? How did I not know about this man before? I was kind of excited to meet him. I mean our Husband was amazing, so his brother had to also be amazing right?

The day came to meet him. My excitement was noticeable about meeting him. I made sure to wear the right clothes and fix my hair. I wanted to make a good impression. We drove into the city to meet up. He was going to take us to walk the strip. We were going to take in some sights and have dinner with him and all the girls.

When we parked and got out of the rental, he was already in the parking lot. He stuck his hand out as he introduced himself to me. His hands were soft, and his voice was stern. He attempted to squeeze my hand as he was shaking it, but I moved my hand out of his quickly. Touching another man didn't seem right even if it was just a handshake. I also felt a little uneasy about him, something wasn't right.

(Let's call him Dave) Dave was boastful of his knowledge, talking about where he had worked and what he had gone to school for. He was self-absorbed. He was also very sure of himself with sister.

I soon realized this man called himself our Husband's brother but was not. They were just friends from the past. At one point in their lives they were apparently very close. I hadn't heard of him, so I was guessing they weren't as close as before.

Dave gave me a vibe, making my skin crawl. I couldn't put my finger on it, but I was sure he wasn't all he was telling me about. I kept him at a distance and never took my eye off him while we were out.

As he talked, I noticed some of his mannerisms were familiar. I learned he went to college with our Husband and sister. He knew both for quite some time. I also learned he was the best man in their wedding. I guess our Husband was close to him at one point. I learned Dave had issues with his heart and had to slow life down a bit. He missed a trip with our Husband several years ago when his heart started acting up again and then they just seemed to lose touch.

It still bothered me that I had never heard of Dave. Why didn't I know Dave existed? Why hadn't our Husband mentioned him before? I was going to ask sister about it when we all got back to the house. I just had to know.

Returning to the house, we ordered dinner, and the girls gathered their items for nightly routines. Dinner was short and we ate together so I couldn't ask her about Dave. The girls were talking so much about what we saw while we were out, I never had a second to talk to sister in-between their conversations.

I decided to wait until it was bedtime. Sister and I shared a room, and all the girls were in a separate room. As they were getting ready for bed my sister wife looked at her phone. She asked if I would like to go out on the town with Dave.

He was sending her messages. Wanting to go out? Why so late? I refused stating I was too tired and needed rest, reminding her the gymnastics meet was in two days. She giggles and tells me she didn't need the rest. She looked at her phone, her car had arrived and out the door she went.

I laid in bed for hours waiting for her to return. What could she be doing at five a.m.? I reminded myself we were in "Sin City" and there were plenty of activities no matter what time. I was aggravated with her because she was being selfish with her time. We had girls there and they should have been the priority.

I heard the front door open. The sun was thinking about coming up by this time. My sister wife attempted to be quiet when she came into our room. She was anything but quiet, but I was still awake waiting. She began to undress, and I found it odd she was taking off her panties.

I sat straight up in bed at this point and looked right at her. She was stunned at my movement. I questioned her about her taking off her panties and she just looked at me. I knew at this point she had fucked our Husbands "brother." As I said it out loud, she knew she was caught.

She began to giggle as if it was funny, and act like some little schoolgirl who got caught fucking in the janitor's closet. I am sure she realized I was in a state of shock when she looked up because her giggling stopped. She then exclaimed the girls could not find out nor could our Husband.

Seriously? She fucked our Husband's closest friend. One he called "brother"? What kind of person does this? How could she? How could he?

That day, the girls requested to go shopping after their schoolwork was finished. While we were out, my sister wife spent a lot of time and a lot of money on my daughter Raven.

It was like the day was all about Raven and what she wanted. I knew at this point it was what my sister wife felt as payment for my silence. She showered Raven knowing I would feel indebted to her for the gifts.

Was this the new way of getting what she wanted? Going through Raven to get to me? Using Raven for my allegiance was just heinous. I always cave when it comes to Raven. This meant I couldn't tell our Husband or Raven would suffer.

It was time to leave the city that never sleeps and go home. I was ready to go because nothing good happened during this trip. I felt trapped at this point. I wasn't sure what to do other than put Raven first and hope nothing else happened that I had to compromise myself for. I was hoping at this point I never had to tell our Husband.

BACK HOME BACK TO SOLITUDE OR SERVITUDE

Back home and back to regular routines was welcomed because I could put myself in my room and not deal with daily harshness or screaming.

Their youngest, Eve, (I called her Eve because her mom always said she was the root cause of all the issues/evil) was trying my patience. She was mean and rude not just to me but to everyone. The day she slapped her mom in the face I almost fell over.

I tried to figure out what caused her to throw such fits of rage, but sister would tell me she was born that way. Sister would say she was born evil, and she never wanted her in the first place. She said it was our Husband's fault Eve was bad and how he should have never forced her to have the kids. She said she hated kids and never wanted any of them.

There were times Eve would just pick a person in the house, and it was their day to be hit and spit on. Not sure if she decided at random or drew names out of a hat but I was ready for our Husband to be home to maybe control it somewhat.

She had physically injured me to the point I had to see a doctor and then a physical therapist. I thought she had broken a bone at one point. I later had to have surgery to repair the damage Eve had caused.

Sister began picking fights with Eve almost daily. I wasn't sure if it was to keep Eve off my back or to be punished when the girls weren't home. I never really thought about sister enjoying the unrest, but I should have.

One evening she began to talk about how Eve was so out of control she would end up in prison because of her actions and words. Her expectations of Eve were low. The thing I noticed while she was saying those things was the smile on her face. Why was she smiling while talking about her own daughter? I turned around and there stood Eve.

I saw Eve's face begin to fade into a place I had seen before. One of sadness. I demanded my wife shut her mouth. She leaned in and told me she would if I would spank her in front of the girls. The look on her face was very sincere but the smirk she gave me told me she wasn't kidding.

I remembered back to the night I was pretending to sleep. The night she talked about the things that turned her on and being spanked in front of the girls was one of them. I had to do this in order to stop the place Eve was going in her mind. I had to do it for Eve.

I yanked the drawer open and grabbed the metal spatula out of the drawer. I grabbed my wife's shirt and pulled with such force I ripped it. My swing of the spatula was swift and hard. As it hit her, she fell to her knees and screamed in pain or pleasure, I didn't care.

Trista immediately jumped up and yelled "one." I knew she wanted to count, and I knew my wife was looking for her to watch. This is what she wanted. She wanted me to spank her while they watched and counted. I was angry because of the words she used to hurt Eve, but I continued to give her what she was asking for.

Eve asked me to stop but I couldn't. I was doing this for her. If I stopped, sister would continue to use her words to hurt Eve. Eve did not understand that I loved her. I loved her more than her mother ever thought about loving her. I would never tell Eve, but I had to do this to ensure she wouldn't be hurt any more today.

Our Husband called later in the day. As I talked with him, I explained I wasn't sure if I was going to be able to handle living in his home much longer. He reminded me of how short the time he was away was becoming. He begged me to be patient and wait for him to be home. I told him I would do my best and I had hoped time would fly by. When we hung up, I sat on the front porch alone and cried.

There were days I would sit and talk with Eve about her mother's behaviors. I explained she had the right to walk away from an argument if it did not pertain to her. If her mother tried to pull her in, she was allowed to not engage with her.

Eve and I both put this into force the following day when sister came home from work angry. She began to yell at Eve about something that didn't pertain to her. I told Eve to go to her room. She began walking to the stairs and sister demanded she stop. When Eve stopped at the bottom of the staircase, I calmly instructed her to continue to her room.

When Eve reached her room, she slammed the door. Sister began to yell at me and tell me I should have stayed out of it. I tried to explain the behaviors she was demonstrating was not because of Eve but something else and Eve was not going to suffer. Sister became even angrier, telling me it was our Husband's fault she had to deal with Eve and again reminded me he had forced her to have children. How she never wanted to be a mother and never wanted kids. I was hoping the girls couldn't hear her but, I think the neighbors could. She was so loud.

Later in the evening, I could hear sister telling our Husband how I stepped in and did not allow her to punish Eve. I could only hear my sister's side of the conversation, but I knew he was telling her he would send me back if she wanted. She was telling him she loved me and wanted me there, but I needed to learn these were her kids not mine and she was to do what she wanted with them or to them.

Sister was making it sound like the girls were not people but possessions. I felt so bad for them. How could anyone act this way? Why would anyone be so cruel to a person they gave birth to? Why was she so determined to drive her kids away from her? Did she really hate them? Did our Husband really force her to have children? All these questions and not one answer.

I started thinking about the time I had met my sister wife's mother and the more I thought about her, the more I realized my sister wife had no idea how to be a mother. I had to show her. I had to talk to her about it. If Eve was ever going to have a chance at a respectful, happy life I needed to make her mother feel loved and how to love herself. Sister was never shown how to love someone or how to love herself.

BEING MOTHERLY

I tried so hard to help my sister wife when it came to being a mother. Her mother never really cared for her, and her father was an angry man who drank until he passed out most nights. It's all sister knew, and I needed to show her it was all wrong.

I would talk to her about the things she would say in front of girls and how it could cause them pain and sadness. There were times she would talk to me and look as if she was listening to what I was saying. Other times she was just blank. Like what I was saying wasn't registering with her.

We had conversations on several occasions about how she treated Eve differently than the others. Sister became agitated with me and made it clear she never wanted Eve. Our Husband made her have Eve. She then went on a lengthy rant about how she never wanted children and how he forced her to have them. All she wanted was to work and advance her career, but he refused to allow her to have what she wanted. In the same breath, she yelled at me about how our Husband forced her to join the Air Force and be a lawyer. Sister said she never wanted to be a lawyer; she had always wanted to be a doctor.

I did everything I could to calm her down. Her yelling made everyone tense. Plus, I didn't want the girls to hear her. She didn't care. She yelled at me and said she was just going to kill herself so we would all be happier. I again asked to stop but she just kept going. Sister began to throw things while she was screaming. I was scared, really scared. She screamed about how she was divorcing our Husband, how she was going to kill herself and it would be Eve's fault because she's evil and how she hated being a mother.

Trista came down the stairs in tears because she could hear what her mom was saying. I walked her back upstairs and asked her to stay in her room until I could calm sister down. Trista looked at me with tears rolling down her face and asked me why her mom was so unhappy all the time and why she was always saying she wanted to kill herself. I didn't have a good answer for Trista, but I hugged her and told her I was doing everything I could to calm sister and hopefully change her behavior.

She calmed down a bit and sat on the couch by the time I came downstairs. Sister's next few words were very confusing to me. She looked at me and told me she was angry at our Husband because he refused to let her be a "Stay at Home Mom" (SAHM) and that was why she was having such difficulty with Eve and all her girls.

OK, I was so confused. She had just told me she never wanted kids and now she is mad because all she ever wanted was to be a SAHM. So, which was it? She was not making any sense. She ranted for over twenty minutes about how she hated being a mom and now she's mad because she can't be one 24/7?

When I asked her to clarify what she was saying she threw her phone and started yelling again. Sister was mad at me because I questioned her. She was making no sense; it was like she was someone completely different. I decided it was time to take the kids out for a walk and to let her get herself together. There was no reason for the kids to hear what she was saying. The girls had been hurt enough for one day.

I won't give up at this point, but my stress level was hitting close to the limit. While I walked with the girls I began to wonder if sister was mentally ill. Did she have more than one personality? Did she have an explosive disorder or was she bipolar? One thing was for sure, she needed some serious mental help. Help she would probably refuse because of her military status and her security clearance.

OUR HUSBAND IS HOME

So many things happened before our Husband came home. I wasn't sure I would be the same person he left. I missed him so much and I needed someone there to help me with sister.

I was so happy when he did get home. His company was exactly what I needed. His smile was so soft and sincere, and I couldn't wait to feel his arms around me. He was calm in the storm I was suffering. Or so I thought.

Day two of him being home everyone was tense and on edge. Sister seemed to be short tempered with everyone. Nothing our Husband did made sister happy even if it was exactly what she asked him to do. Then it happened.

Eve came in the door and began yelling immediately at her mother about something she was lacking for her gym requirements. She walked by her mother and hit her hands, flinging all the items she had in her hand up in the air. Sister yelled at Eve and Eve slapped sister in the face. I was standing in the kitchen, shocked at the events that had just occurred.

Eve then ran to the back door where our Husband was standing. He grabbed her and began to hit her (like a dad would spank his kids) rather aggressively. I ran to the back door and pulled them apart. Getting in between them and pushing them apart.

I sent Eve to her room and pulled our Husband outside. I had him sit in a chair and gather himself. I explained to him we don't hit in this house or put our hands on anyone in anger. He looked at me like I was speaking in a language he had never heard.

I continued with all the things that had changed since he had been gone. We talked about how Eve has been trying to walk away from sister when she is in a crabby mood and how when we use our words, we do so calmly.

I also told him I understood how he felt when he told me it was difficult to integrate back into a family after being gone for so long. Life didn't stop when he left, it kept moving. Coming home, it's hard to catch up with all the changes and it can be frustrating.

At dinner that night, we all sat and tried to talk about things in the house and what has changed for everyone. One of the things that had changed was, each person spoke at dinner and told something about their day.

This was a way for everyone to keep up with what has happened in the many lives in the house. It also made each of the girls feel as if what they had to say was important, not just to them but to everyone.

Later that week it was announced where our Husband would be next and it wasn't where we all were living. It was in a neighboring state, but it still felt as if it was halfway around the world to me. The only good news was I was going to be going with him to help him find a place to live while he was there. Several days with him alone and I couldn't wait. I needed some alone time with our Husband and I deserved it.

It did make me sad when the thought of him not being home was going to be the result. I put that thought to the side though and enjoyed the fact that he and I were going to spend several days without anyone interrupting. Furthermore, his new duty station was going to be close enough he could come home on the weekends.

This would mean sharing him on the weekends with everyone but that was OK. I had hoped he would put the kids first and his wives second. I also must put these thoughts out of my mind and focus on the task at hand. Preparing for my alone time.

Getting ready for several days with my love was all I could think about. Although my dad was sick, I could still feel the excitement all the way down to my toes. I was so happy, and it was noticeable to everyone.

Our Husband was excited too. He talked about all the things we could do while we were there other than looking for a place for him to live. He did pull me to the side to ask about my dad to make sure I still wanted to go. I knew my dad was not well, but I assured him I had talked to Jade, and she made it clear there was nothing I could do other than watch dad sleep.

A few days into the apartment hunting, we were laying in bed. Jade called; my dad had died. I looked at our Husband and he knew. I cried for what seemed like hours while our Husband held me. I was devastated. I loved my dad so much. Our Husband sat and listened to all the funny, sad and silly stories about my dad that night and for the rest of the time we were there. Right up to the time I left to go home for his funeral. I just couldn't talk about how wonderful my dad was and how I was going to miss him dearly.

OUR HUSBAND IS GONE AGAIN

It was moving day for our Husband. I was still sad over the passing of my dad, and this wasn't helping. It was a sad day for most of us but sister didn't seem to be bothered by it. This new adventure was going to take a toll on me for sure. I am at the house again without him for days on end, feeling alone.

My sister wife and I were beginning to get along better. She was trying to take things in stride but also did things she needed to be punished for. Most of the time it was intentional which made me want to punish her harder.

I was getting to the point I felt she deserved to be punished. She treated everyone as if they were beneath her. This is what she was teaching the girls, especially Eve. Why would she want Eve to walk around acting like she was entitled? Didn't she know people hated people who acted that way?

Even though Eve and her mother fought constantly it was teaching her how to put others down just to make herself feel better. The longer I watched her teaching Eve these behaviors the more I wanted to beat her into submission. I didn't want Eve to grow up and act like her mother.

It had been several weeks since our Husband had moved and then all hell broke loose in the house. Doors were being slammed and hateful words from the girls were spewing out of their mouths. What has happened and will I make it three more days to the weekend?

SO MUCH STUFF SO LITTLE TIME

All the girls in the house got into an argument over rumors and gossip. How did this happen and where did this start? I was determined to get to the bottom of this and stop all the hate being thrown around the house.

I found out the conflict involved a mutual friend they all talked to. This girl was the daughter of the "third" wife. Something wasn't adding up and I really needed to find out what was going on. It wasn't the first time this girl caused problems with us or other families from the previous gym.

I separated everyone at this point and took my sister wife into the bedroom for a bit of conversation. I was going to tell her it involved this girl and what I had found out so far. While talking with her, I made her get the clamps out of the punishment bag and a set of balls. She chose the balls and inserted them into her pussy after she wet them with her mouth.

Now, time for conversation. When I started telling sister about this girl texting our girls with rumors and trash talk, sister began to get angry. Seeing as our Husband and my sister wife both have names that start with the same first four letters, it's very easy to type in the first few letters and send a message. Sometimes it may go to the wrong spouse because of this. That's when things confuse them. When I sent a message to him that was meant for her, he would be confused, wanting to know what I was talking about. It happened a lot.

Obviously, I wasn't the only person who had this issue when

sending texts to one or the other of them. The third wife also had an issue with this and happened to send a selfie to my sister wife that was intended for our Husband. When she showed it to me, she started explaining things to me in a sequence of events. The picture, the girls fighting, the phone calls and name calling. Everything was starting to make sense.

Sister walked out of the bedroom and started to talk. I stopped her and asked that Eve leave the room. This did not pertain to her. Only Trista and Raven were fighting, and it needed to be settled. Eve didn't need to see what we were about to show the other girls.

When Eve was out of sight and in her room, she placed her phone on the table between Trista and Raven, with the picture on the screen. They looked very confused until she exclaimed with a raised voice, "She is trying to steal my husband!"

Sister realized she shouldn't have raised her voice because she felt the balls, the ones she had inserted into her pussy earlier slip a little. She had to excuse herself to fix her problem. All I could say to her was, we don't yell in the house.

While sister was in the bathroom, I looked at Trista and Raven staring at the picture. Raven looked at me and asked me why the "third" wife would be sending naked pictures of herself with her hand spreading her pussy open to sister's phone. I explained to her and Trista how easy it was to mix up the numbers and how the picture was meant for our Husband.

When sister came out of the bathroom, conversation with the two girls took most of the night and there were lots of tears. It seems the "third" wife and her daughter were trying to split the family. They almost accomplished it. I was happy we were in a place of growth where we could all sit and talk instead of walking away. I hugged both of them when it was over and they went

93

upstairs to talk.

My sister wife and I talked alone as well. She was hiding this from me for quite some time. I was not happy. I wasn't sure who to be angry with, my sister wife, our Husband or the woman who wanted to be the third. Not only was I angry, but I was also very hurt by all three of them.

Talking with my sister wife , she began to tell me how our Husband was being obstinate, refusing to talk with her about family issues or their relationship. I wasn't sure how to help so I asked her what I could do to make things better for her. The entire time we talked, it was all about how our Husband wouldn't comply with what she wanted. Not one time did she ask me how I was or if I was OK. It was about sister getting her way or else.

Sister wife made it clear our Husband could see a therapist or their marriage was over. She said she wasn't sure she wanted to stay with him anyway. He made her miserable and when Eve turned eighteen, she was filing for divorce so what did it matter if she started now? She continued ranting about how he wouldn't do what she wanted and being divorced was the only way sister was going to be happy.

I asked again how I could help but she didn't have an answer other than to get our Husband out of her space. I told her he would be home in a few days, and we could all talk. I told her until then, she didn't have to think about our Husband or the naked, vulgare picture from the "third." I had her calm, her breathing had slowed so I told her she needed to go to bed.

The next day was calmer with the girls but still not where it should have been. They were so good just weeks ago. I had to figure more of this out before our Husband came home. Even though I had a terrible feeling about the whole incident, I didn't want matters to get worse by our Husband getting angry.

I called her. The third wife deserved to give her side and I was ready to ask all the questions. She and I were so close at one point, and I really needed her to tell me it was an accident. Instead, she did not deny sending pictures to our Husband. She in fact admitted to sending the pictures to him on more than one occasion. She also admitted to sending videos to him of her doing inappropriate things for him to masturbate to. I was dying inside. She was my friend.

What I didn't expect was the videos she sent to me. The ones our husband sent to her. As I watched the videos of him stroking his cock and saying her name over and over, just the way he used to send to me, my heart fell. I was so hurt. So hurt I had no words to describe it.

I didn't sleep with sister that night. I knew better. She would see right through me and know I wasn't telling her something. I cried myself to sleep that night on the couch, alone.

By the time our Husband got home that Friday evening, sister was furious. I didn't tell her about the videos he had sent the third. I couldn't tell her because I had been working on them communicating with each other since I moved to their house. Sister already wanted a divorce and hated our Husband; I couldn't make it worse.

Why does she hate him so much? Why is she always telling me how much she despises him? Why is she always so verbally and mentally abusive to him? I was determined to find out because I loved them both. The love for each was a bit different than the other but I loved them both. I set my heart and feelings to the side and decided I was going to do what I could to repair the damage the third had done.

After dinner, the adults went outside to the back patio. It was time for us to talk about the pictures that were sent and what exactly happened. Before anyone said anything, I made it clear there was not yelling or name calling. This was to be a civil conversation.

Our Husband put his head down as she began to talk to him about what had happened with the text mix-up. She was angry. She started to raise her voice and I put my hand on her knee.

She looked at me and I calmly said to her, "We all do things we wish we hadn't and not everything we've done are things we are proud of. So, I think we all need to take a breath and relax for a minute and talk like rational adults."

Sister wife sat back in her chair because she knew I was talking about our Husband's fake brother who betrayed everyone and fucked her while we were out of town. I had to stop thinking about it before I got mad. She then allowed our Husband to speak and attempt to defend himself.

I sat there while he apologized to her over and over. He looked sorry and he sounded sorry, but was he? He apologized for looking at those photos of the third and swore it was nothing to him and nothing to worry about. He blamed it on the third, always being drunk and out of control.

I sat there while he didn't really lie to her but didn't tell her the entire truth either. This was just as if he were lying. He wasn't sorry, if he were, he would tell her the whole truth. All of it, not just the parts she already knew. I was screaming in my head, begging him to come clean and do the right thing. Crying for him to be the man I thought he was but no, it didn't happen.

He had no idea I knew the truth or at least more than he was admitting to sister. Why was he doing this? Did he not really love her or care? Was he hiding other affairs from her? From me? I had to stop my mind before I went over the edge and my face or mouth would tell what I was thinking.

After the conversation was over and sister was satisfied with what he had told her she went back inside the house. I just sat there, looking at him waiting for more words to come out. Waiting for him to admit what he did and beg me to forgive him.

I asked him if there was anything more, he had to say for himself as I looked him right in the eye. He started to open his mouth and I stopped him from talking. I told him before he started to repeat the story he gave our wife, I asked him if there was anything else. I then made it clear I probably already knew the answer.

He began to cry because he knew I knew. He apologized over and over to me for not telling the whole story in the beginning. I did what I could to not cry but I couldn't stop myself.

I sat outside for over an hour crying while he watched and tried to make me feel better. I was too hurt and too angry to listen at this point. I also told him our trust was broken and it was up to him to fix it. I wasn't going to just roll over like sister did and walk away. He had to prove he was not going to lie and break my trust again. I don't hand it out freely and if it's broken it's not my job to repair it.

He had a long road ahead of him to make this up to me and what makes it even harder is, I didn't know at this point but there was more to the third he later revealed. He didn't tell me the truth while I sat there and cried. I thought he was sorry but he wasn't.

SISTER WIFE HAS TO MOVE

Orders came in and it was now time for sister to move. The girls all went from homeschool to public school and had friends. None of them wanted to move. Since the house we were in was close to the middle of where my spouses were going to be they decided to keep it and leave me and all the girls there.

Sister wife moved to her next station without any issues and our Husband helped her. I was nervous about keeping Eve alone and my nerves were getting the best of me. Because of this, sister was about to get a punishment.

I sent her a text and all it said was "braid your hair." It was going to be my gift to her to look at all week while she was in her new place, and I was home with all the girls. Her excitement was clear as she jumped up off the couch and left the room with a smile on her face.

I waited a bit before I went into our room. As I walked in, I announced I was going to shower and shut the door. I made sure to lock the door because sister was already naked, face down on the bed.

I grabbed my phone and Bluetooth speaker. I like my music loud while I shower and everyone in the house knows this. I turned it up as I made sister wife pick her punishment tool of choice.

I do this sometimes because I remember thinking about having to get a switch off the tree. The anticipation of carrying it back to your punishment place was torture. I was going to make her look at it while I showered to add a little punishment to what she was about to get.

She chose a riding crop and handed it to me. I connected my phone to the speaker and turned it up. I laid the crop on the bed in front of her and walked into the bathroom to shower.

When I finished my shower, I walked back into the bedroom. Sister was still face down on the bed looking at the crop. I then shoved a balled-up cloth in her mouth and tied it there with a scarf. I would hate for anyone to hear her screams.

I used some long calf socks (our Husband's) to tie her hands and feet. Moving was not allowed during punishment time without further consequences. I picked up the crop and looked at it. Was I starting to enjoy punishing her? Why? I loved her and wanted her to be happy. Maybe because this is what makes her happy. I brushed the dark thoughts off and justified it by telling myself it was for sister's happiness.

The first hit landed hard on her right ass cheek and instantly left a raised red mark. Sister let out a small noise, that was all she could do since I had bound her mouth. I repeated this until she begged me to stop and then I repeated it several more times because talking or making noise was not permitted. Sister knew this and knew it meant more punishment.

By the time I was done with her, her entire ass and upper thighs were red and, in some places, even bruised. Before I let her up, I asked her if she knew why she was being punished.

She replied, "No, ma'am."

She knew she had to give me an answer. She knew punishment continued until she could tell me why she was being punished in the first place. This caused her to get more until she could tell me why she was being punished.

She was finally able to tell me that leaving me with all the kids alone was the reason. That I will be dealing with all the issues they had and correcting behaviors. That Eve would do everything she could to make me hate my life and I would have to do it all alone. I listened to sister while she was talking but I was looking at the blood trickling down to her inner thigh.

I grabbed her braid, pulled her head back to where she leaned her entire body back and slammed the crop into her tits so hard it instantly made her nipples erect. I let go and her head fell to the bed. I untied her hands and told her to untie the rest of her restraints herself and to clean herself up.

I walked back into the bathroom and showered again while she was cleaning up and putting things away. I hated getting sweaty especially after a shower. She finished and walked into the bathroom and asked for permission to leave the room. I told her if she did not put my things away properly it was going to be another punishment when I got out of the shower. Sister assured me it was all put away in the proper places.

After my shower we loaded the rest of her things in her car. She left the following day and headed to her new station. This was the beginning of a fresh start for her while I stayed to clean up her mess. The more I thought about it, the more I wanted to beat her again.

TEEN GIRLS ARE TOUGH

The months following both my spouses leaving were rough with the girls. COVID had hit at one point and all kinds of things changed. Some for the good, others for the worse.

Eve was getting better at showing her true self. A side I hadn't seen in her before. She smiled more and laughed a lot. Her and Raven began to get along well. They spent a lot of time together painting and doing other various things. I liked this side of her, but I knew it wouldn't last. All it would take was sister coming home.

When things began to relax a bit and her mom was able to return, the old Eve began to show up. All she wanted was her mother to love her and show approval. Her mom didn't have time for that, she was too busy playing games on her phone or working to even talk to Eve. This brought out the worst in Eve.

These things also made Trista feel bad. She was already on medications for depression and seeing a shrink. She had so many anxiety issues. Trista was taking double the dose of sleeping aids and still not resting.

When I would ask Eve and Trista why they refused to talk to their mom and tell her how they felt to possibly make things better for them, they both began to cry. Trista said her mom would never understand and even if she did, she would tell us how much worse her life is and that she is sick and can't deal with it.

Sister was always sick. I started thinking about what Trista had said and it was then I realized, if someone around sister was diagnosed with something sister also had it. I could see where Trista was coming from. Her mom faked migraines all the time. She would drag her leg behind her like a dead weight and blame her migraine.

OK, I know its comical to imagine her doing the leg drag but it was sad she would do this in order to avoid her kids or something else she just refused to deal with.

Side note, I had to video her at one point for her new doctor when her migraine symptoms showed up. She told me on a Saturday morning about it and within thirty minutes, BAM! We had a migraine. I took her phone and hit the record button. She sagged the side of her face to make it look like she was having a stroke. She then walked towards me dragging her one leg behind her. I held my breath because I was about to laugh. When she got close enough, I told her I stopped the recording, and I was sure I had gotten enough for her new doctor to see. Just as fast as those symptoms started, they stopped! She walked over to me normally, thanked me and walked away as if nothing had happened. WTF?

Anyway, back to Trista. She was such a sad person. I would get her out of her room and involved in things, but it only lasted a short time. She was obviously looking for something to bring a little bit of happiness into her life, but nothing was working for her.

Not being at the school was making her worse. Stupid COVID. She was missing those she passed in the hallway and all the distractions she used to mask her sadness.

One Friday afternoon Trista was invited over to a friend's house to play video games. She and this guy apparently shared a love for a particular game. She sent a text to her mom first asking her if it was OK for her to go, due to some of the COVID regulations relaxing and her mom said it was a great idea. When she asked me, she never mentioned it was a guy. I didn't have any issues with her spending time with friends, so I also allowed her to go.

I was hoping Trista would feel better by getting out of the house and seeing a friend. I was worried about her and her depression. Depression can do things to a person and none of those things are good. When Trista got home, she went upstairs and straight to her room. I went up later to see how she was, but she was sleeping so I left her alone. It wasn't odd for her to sleep for fifteen hours so I didn't worry when she didn't come down for dinner.

Saturday morning hit me like a ton of bricks. There was early practice for Raven and work for Trista and something Eve had to do so they were all going to be out of the house. I decided going back to bed after they all headed out the door was a great idea.

Each girl stuck their head in my room before they left to tell me they were leaving, and they loved me. It was normal and I loved it even if I was tired and waiting to go back to bed.

This morning was a bit different, and I couldn't put my finger on it. Not until a few minutes later when Trista poked her head back in my room. She looked a little sad and confused. I told her to come in and have a seat on the bed, I was there to listen. When she sat down, tears flowed from her eyes instantly. She began to ask questions about sex. What it was supposed to feel like and how it was supposed to happen.

The questions about sex kept up and they were very specific. I had to ask her, because if she did lose her virginity, I wanted to make sure she was OK.

The more she described what had happened the more it

103

sounded like rape. She said she initially was hesitant to say yes but he kept putting his hands on her begging for her to let him. Even with her telling him she wasn't comfortable he continued anyway.

The more she talked the angrier I was. He knew she was just the right victim out of the three girls because she had a difficult time saying no. He knew she felt like she wasn't enough for her mother, and she didn't feel loved because she talked to him. He was supposed to be her friend. He was a predator, and she was the perfect victim.

I, of course, ran to the pharmacy to get a Plan B and had her take it immediately. I sat with her the rest of the day, and the first thing Monday morning, I called the doctor to get her in. Thankfully, all her tests came back negative for STD's, but the doctor said they must be repeated in a few months. How am I going to explain this to her parents?

Of course, the doctor had to notify the police because she is a minor. When the police showed up to talk with her, she refused. I told her she had to at least tell them herself she didn't want to talk and give them permission to talk to me so I could deescalate the situation. Trista poked her head out of the door and told the detective she wasn't talking, and I could answer all her questions.

The detective wasn't happy about Trista not talking but I stepped outside and sat in one of the rocking chairs on the porch. The detective was dressed in plain clothes, and she spoke softly about why she was there. As we talked, I sensed she was wanting to ask me something specific. I finally looked at her and asked her what she wanted to know. She explained to me how this report landed on her desk and that she thought she was looking for someone who was trafficking young girls. She was there in hopes of catching a sex trafficker. I almost got arrested for sex trafficking because of this situation. Thankfully she believed me, and I didn't go to jail. Now was the hard part, no telling the other girls and her parents.

She begged and begged, I finally caved and said OK. I would keep all the events to myself for the time being. I agreed with stipulations. She must talk to me daily, even when she left for college, she had to at least text me daily to let me know she was handling her feelings. With her depression, I couldn't chance her doing anything to hurt herself. I figured with Karma coming to town, I would have a distraction and not think about what had happened.

Karma arrived that afternoon and I picked her up at the airport. I had to tell her the secret I had been carrying for the last five days. I didn't have a therapist, but I needed one. Karma was my only outlet, and I knew she would never tell a soul. She told me I had to respect Trista's wishes and not tell anyone even though I felt she needed therapy. I knew she was right, I had to keep quiet if Trista kept her end of the deal.

The second night Karma was there, Raven came down to my room and showed me a text from the same guy who had assaulted Trista on her phone. It was one thirty in the morning and this guy wanted Raven to come outside. Was she to be his next victim? Hell no! Karma and I went out with Raven's phone and waited. He parked a block away and walked up from the neighbor's yard where it was dark. When he was close enough to see us, I spoke. When I say we scared the shit out of him I seriously think he may have shat his pants.

I decided at that point, Trista had to tell Raven so she could protect herself and Eve at school. I was sure he would go after Eve next. Eve was also an easy target because she just wanted attention and someone to love her. Raven had to be told.

Trista's talk with Raven wasn't easy. They both cried and Raven promised to be there for her anytime she needed her. Raven made it clear she was going to always be there for her, and she would do whatever Trista needed. It was nice to see my girl being so thoughtful and grown. She then made it a point to let this guy know, she knew what he did and if he got anywhere near Eve, she would destroy him.

Thankfully we had zero incidents with him for the rest of their high school careers. We were then able to keep things a secret from her parents like she asked of me and off to college Trista went. She promised to keep me in the loop in her life so I would know she wasn't spiraling out of control.

I was still scared for her because I knew she was the world's best liar. I watched Trista so many times look her parents in the face and lie right through her teeth. I knew the truth and I would almost believe the lie. She was good, that's for sure.

Then the other two, Raven and Eve were to begin their senior year in high school. I was ready for a little bit of calm before the summer's end which was not anywhere near what was coming for me. Things were about to get a bit crazier.

ALONG CAME A WEDDING

It seems the oldest of the girls, most of my family and friends referred to her as "the Mormon one", (Rebecca) was to marry this summer. I had to listen to sister complain about her and her Mormon fiancée. Not only was she saying it was a cult, but sister's father also talked and talked about how it was a cult.

Sister's father tried to convince everyone Rebecca had joined a cult. He was concerned for Rebecca's safety and couldn't understand how her parents would let her ruin her life by being in a cult.

I literally know nothing about the Mormon religion. I could care less one way or another about what religion people are. If they are nice to me, I'll be nice to you.

The weekends with sister wife were very stressful. She would complain about how Rebecca would sit on the "circle couch" and her and the fiancée would suck face all day. It was disgusting and made her want to throw up. Sister would rant about how they were basically dry fucking on the circle couch and the only reason they wanted to marry was because they wanted to fuck all the time.

Sister wife made it clear she was going to keep acting crazy until they were out of her apartment and away from her. I told her they grow so fast, and she should appreciate the time she has with her kids before they leave for the last time. All sister had to say about it was how she couldn't wait to have an empty nest so she could be alone. She usually added "with you" when she was talking to me.

Alone? With me? I was confused by this statement especially when she would add me to the mix. It was also something she was saying more and more as time went on. Was she serious when she said she was divorcing our Husband? I decided I would watch her closer to see if there were any other behaviors she had changed in the recent past.

I learned quickly sister was not happy about the marriage but said she would pretend. She said she was feeling the same as her father but didn't want anyone else to know. I felt this was her father talking and how he hated the cult his granddaughter was drug into. After talking with sister a few times, I realized she was angry because she felt Rebecca was being brainwashed and her Mormon husband was going to ruin her.

I talked with our Husband about the upcoming wedding and what it meant to him. He was worried of course but wanted Rebecca to be happy. He felt she was also jumping into a marriage because her fiancée's family was forcing the issue and they just wanted to fuck.

I told him my concerns about the upcoming marriage and what I thought was pressing. It was mostly about Rebecca for me. I had nothing against her intended, but I worried about her and her heart condition and how he was going to take care of her. Rebecca was coming from a military family who had full insurance on her with no out of pocket expenses. Was he going to be able to make sure she was going to be OK? Those were my questions.

It seemed when I asked sister about it, she would tell me it wasn't her problem and this was a choice Rebecca was making for herself. Did she not care if Rebecca could see a doctor or go to the ER without stressing about how to pay for it if she had a heart incident? I was terrified for Rebecca only because of this issue. I wanted her to be able to get the medical help she needed. I wanted her happy, but I also wanted her to be healthy.

Finally, our Husband said he would take my concerns and talk with Rebecca about it. I felt better after he told me it was something he asked her to do before the big day. Find health insurance she could afford that covered her. I was thankful he talked with Rebecca and set some guidelines for her to meet.

I continued to talk with sister throughout the summer about the wedding even with COVID being all crazy. Mostly through texts and phone conversations. Sister continued to complain about Rebecca and her man being in her apartment all the time making a mess and not picking up after themselves. When sister said dry fucking on the circle couch and moaning, that did it for me and I busted out laughing.

I'm not sure what day they married or what day the fake wedding was in front of the parents of each one and the wedding party. (There was also another fake thing at a Mormon church or his parents' house that I'll get to later.) I just knew they were married and finally in an apartment that wasn't sisters.

We all stayed in a hotel for the fake wedding where sister had her apartment. I felt like I spent most of my time calming sister and punishing her. She was on a rampage most of the time we were all getting ready. I did what I could to keep her calm and to keep her from yelling. She kept trying to make the day about her and it was making me angry.

There were several times I would pinch sister for saying something rude. She would wince but smile when she looked at me. There was also another time she had Trista count while all the girls watched. The girls giggled but sister knew she was in trouble later. This time was about Rebecca not her.

When we were able to get all the girls ready, sister went to her room to get her dress on. I decided to wear something casual. I am not a dress up kind of person. I walked out into the hotel hallway as sister was also leaving her room. I was in shock.

Sister looked like she was in a high school homecoming dress. I tried to not let my face say what I was thinking. I kept repeating "keep it together" in my head as sister approached me. When she asked me how she looked, I simply suggested she did not have the corset so tight. She demanded it had to be so her dress wouldn't fall off. I casually replied to her, her back fat made it look like she had back boobs as I snapped a picture to send to my friend back home.

Sister was infuriated and screamed at me to fix it. She started yelling about how she wasn't going to the wedding and how Rebecca was showing off and it was all just dumb. Sister stomped her feet like a toddler and threw all the items in her hand. I picked them up and told her if she ruined this day for Rebecca, she would regret it when I was done with her.

When the formalities were over, I was ready to go home. I wanted to have some calm, some sense of peace, even if it was for five minutes, I needed it!

Sister's father was in a separate room at the hotel and started acting like he was lost. I talked with him for a bit, and I let sister know he was acting strange. Sister told me he was just drunk and needed to stay in his room. It was our last night and he seemed so confused. Sister screamed at him and told him to shut his mouth and stay in his room. She took his keys so he couldn't leave. As we walked away from his room, she mumbled about how she wished he would just die.

Sister decided to come home for a couple of days, and I was ready to sit with her and relax. I was hoping she would calm down and find something positive to say or do while she was home. I asked her if she would like to have some wine outside on the patio.

Sitting outside, glass of wine in hand, sister wife announces her first born is married. She then proceeded to tell me all about how her new son-in-law is addicted to porn and how he would rather watch it than do anything with his life according to Rebecca.

She said Rebecca told her all about how he would watch porn all the time and spend not just hours on end watching but her money just to watch porn. Sister continued with how she was told it was fine with the church because Rebecca was not going to allow him to take any other wives.

I stood up and announced it was a bit late for that type of announcement because they were already married, and it was not my business. When hearing from other people sister had said the same thing to them, I realized sister couldn't keep her mouth shut. I spent so much time doing damage control before it got back to Rebecca.

Even if it was true, the only person sister was hurting was Rebecca and I couldn't allow her to be hurt like this. I confronted sister about this and all she had to say for herself was, she wasn't spreading lies. It was all true and Rebecca should have thought about it before she married into a cult.

I let it go and decided to pick my battles with sister.

WEEKENDS WITH SISTER AND OUR HUSBAND

Spending time together, all three of us, was something I think sister and our Husband enjoyed. It was sometimes difficult for me. Sister wanted her weekly punishments and our Husband wanted to get laid and have a sense of family. I just wanted everyone to get along and stop the violence.

Sister would yell and scream at our Husband regularly. There wasn't a weekend that went by without sister making someone cry. She thrived off the pain of others. I could see it when she caused pain. The smile she tried to hide and the gratification she showed when she felt she won.

At about mid-summer I had enough of her yelling, her rudeness and her fits. I pulled her into the bedroom and asked her what her issue was. She informed me the punishments weren't working and she felt she needed more in order to control herself.

Hurting my feelings was one thing but hurting someone else's feelings is another, especially when I love the one you are hurting. Then to blame me because my punishments were not enough to make her stop? I could feel an anger inside I hadn't felt before.

I grabbed sister's hair and pulled her to the bed. I didn't wait for her to prepare anything, I grabbed her shorts and pulled until one side of her ass cheek was exposed and I smacked her with my hand. This pissed me off even more, my hand was stinging like it hadn't ever stung before.

I reached for the cane and hit the music button on the speaker. Thankfully it was already loud because in the same

112

motion towards the speaker I grabbed the cane and hit her bare skin on the same ass cheek. The force I used to hit her made my hand vibrate, this meant it was harder than usual. I looked and the mark was red and slightly bleeding.

I continued hitting her with the cane and demanded she remove her clothes. I made it clear if she made any noise, her punishment was going to do more than sting and bleed.

She replied, "Yes, ma'am."

I watched her face turn from a light red to a fire red as I raised the cane again. I had to inform her, she made noise, and this was not going to be the last of her punishment. She slammed her face in the pillow and tried not to breathe until I was finished. She was bruised, red and bleeding and she deserved every bit of it.

When I let her up, I pointed to the bathroom. When she walked in, I handed her a tube of cream. She thanked me until she saw what I had handed her. I didn't think her face could get any redder until she realized I had handed her something that was going to burn her already burning skin. I wanted her to feel the pain, I wanted the pain to drag out to the point she couldn't focus.

This is what she wanted from me. Sister did tell me her punishments were not enough and she needed more in order to stay in control of herself. I was just giving her what she wanted from me.

As she applied the cream, I watched. I wanted to make sure she didn't miss a spot. For the rest of the evening, when she sat, stood and shifted or took a step, she would wince in pain. Pain she deserved for hurting others.

I wanted to feel bad, but I didn't. First, our Husband had feelings and she hurt them and second, she asked for it. So, I don't feel bad. I was happy she was in pain this time. I also secretly hoped it hurt for days. The pain she inflicted would hurt those around her for the rest of their lives. It would cause them to be fucked up and need therapy for years.

Our Husband knew what had happened in the bedroom while he was not allowed in. He never wanted to talk about it because his father beat him severely when he was young, and it all brought back memories he didn't want to think about. I felt terrible thinking about all the noises of the beatings and how it affected our Husband. The pain from his father followed him into his adulthood.

Therefore, he was never involved with the beatings. This is what she needed, and he couldn't provide because his childhood was less than perfect with an easily agitated father with a twitchy hand. I understood how he felt, and I hurt for him.

Some of the things that were occurring in this family dynamic were starting to make sense. Our husband was OK with the abuse my sister dished out to him because it was better than being hit on a regular basis by his father. Love was pain for him and if it didn't hurt it wasn't love.

The more I thought about this as the weeks went on and the behaviors didn't change, I wasn't sure I could handle this life. This was all kinds of fucked up and I wasn't sure I could participate in the fuckery much longer.

Talking with our Husband, he explained it would be different when he retired, and the kids were all at college. He could leave the house when sister wanted beat and he would be free to fuck me any time he wanted. He said there would be no more hiding. He could show his feelings for me all he wanted, and sister could act out and be punished daily.

I tried so hard to believe him and I really wanted to. He made it sound so easy. Like sister's mental abuse would be better and all would be fine. I loved him and I loved sister and didn't want to lose either of them.

WHAT ABOUT MY FEELINGS?

They both seemed to fill something I think I was needing in my life at the time. Our Husband was showing me a side of men I had never seen before. He was quiet, complacent almost. He knew his role and knew he would suffer if he was to deviate from his role.

He was me. He was the male version of me when sister was around. He showed every sign of being an abused spouse. He softened my heart when it came to men but only just a little.

I loved him and it made me sad to see him hurting the way he was, but he would need me to be softened in order to get into my heart. Was this sister's idea in order to get me to stay? She already controlled our Husband so was she using him to control me?

My mind was all over the place. I didn't want to be controlled. I wanted to be free. I lived with being controlling before. Therefore, she wanted me to beat her. Why? To make me feel like I had the freedom to choose my life? To make me feel more dominant over her? She controlled our Husband. Did she want me to feel like I controlled her?

No way! Neither of them would do this to me. They loved me. They both told me repeatedly how much they loved me. I felt loved. He provided the softer side of love I needed, and she provided the harsher side where I felt like I was in control. They weren't doing this to harm me because they loved me. Right?

Did they love me and care for me like I loved and cared for

them? For their kids? Of course, they did! I talked with both at separate times about this topic. Why was my head spinning like I had no control over my life? Was it a charade for them? Was I a game?

When talking to sister she would tell me all the time, she would provide for me and Raven and love us like we deserved to be loved. She said we would never want for anything ever. Sister wanted us to be happy and never fear for our safety or wonder where our needs would come from.

When talking to our Husband, he made it clear he would never leave me. He would never leave us, Raven and me. Raven and I will never have to worry about anything. He said he loved Raven like she was his and he loved me like I had been his wife from day one.

This made me love them even more. I was so in love with not one but two people who seemed to only want the best for me. All I could see was the picture they were painting for me. The life I would have with zero worry and all the love I could handle.

ONE MORE YEAR

I decided I was not going to go when it came to taking Trista to college and getting her settled in. I also had decided I wasn't going for parents' weekend like they wanted. I didn't want to be a part of the chaos. Especially with Eve going. It always turned into a war between her and sister for all the attention. Poor Trista, never standing up for herself and allowing everyone to see her as an easy target.

I did however, take Trista shopping and had her grab all she thought she needed for her first year of college. I explained to her there were also going to be things she needed after she got there. Her dad (our Husband) had decided he was going to take her and make it a daddy daughter day. This made her happy which in turn made me happy.

The other two girls were gearing up for their first last day of high school. We were getting closer and closer to the end of me paying my dues. By dues, I mean things like, being hit on several occasions by Eve, listening to Eve call me names and having to separate Eve from sister when they would fight.

Our Husband reminded me his time was almost up and he was out in a matter of months. He reminded me soon after his last day, sister would be going to a new place to finish out her service and she would retire. That's when sister would change and stop being so crazy, our Husband would say. I felt he thought she would just flip a switch and be fine. I hoped he was right and with all the stress of the girls gone she would stop being so out of control.

I knew while she was at her new place, our Husband and I would be sight-seeing the entire area. There was so much to see in the capitol and our Husband talked about all the things he wanted to show me. They had lived there before and knew a lot about the area and he was like a schoolboy when he talked about showing me all the sights.

When sister retired, we were all leaving and traveling all over the world. Sister talked often of the things she had seen across the globe and how she couldn't wait to show me. I didn't care where we were if things were calm, and we were all together.

I talked to sister about the possibility of things being calm once we all moved. Time was getting short, and plans needed to be made. She assured me by moving time, our Husband would be gone because she didn't want to stay married to him. She would say things about Eve turning eighteen and how she had planned on making the divorce official as soon as all the kids were legal adults. Eve being the youngest, it would be her eighteenth birthday.

I would then whisper to myself, "one more year." I wasn't sure if I was trying to convince myself our Husband was right or if I was moving back to my hometown in a year. I just needed to get through it and hope for the best. Our Husband had high hopes and sister had a plan he knew nothing about.

SISTER WIFE HAD IDEAS

Sister was trying her best to get me to agree that our Husband was a bad man. She would tell me how she would try to talk to him and how he would refuse to listen to what she had to say. Sister said he only cared about himself and didn't care what was going on around him if his needs were met.

Sister was also trying to balance too many things at once. I asked her if there was anything I could do to help her. I knew she was stressed and taking anything off her plate would help. When I would ask her, she would throw her hands up and yell she didn't have a clue. Not this time.

This time, she looked me right in my face and asked me to take her "wifely duties" right down to satisfying his bedroom needs. The look on my face was probably one of confusion and disbelief. She said she didn't even want to participate in the bedroom any more.

I tried to tell sister having sex was a stress reliever and she should be having more sex. I felt like I was talking to the palm tree in the front yard. Her face was blank and the only emotion she was showing was anger.

She looked me right in my face and asked me if he (our Husband) ever finished the job. I was a bit confused about what she was asking until she asked me how many times. Was she really asking me this? If faked an orgasm while fucking our Husband?

I was now confused about why she would ask me about

faking. The confusion continued to get worse when she asked me if I would rather make myself cum than fake it with our Husband and have all that cum inside me for nothing. Sister made having sex with our Husband sound like it was a chore rather than something she wanted and enjoyed. Like it was nothing but a problem for her.

Silence. That was all I had for a few minutes. I stared at her in confusion, disbelief, and possibly anger. I couldn't put my finger on the feeling welling up inside my body. I pushed it to the side.

I looked at sister wife and made sure I was hearing her correctly. As I started to repeat the questions, she stopped me. Her expression was what I felt, that of disappointment, anger, and hate.

Sister then exclaimed, "I have never had an orgasm while fucking that man my entire life with him. All twenty plus years of fucking that man and not one time has he ever made me cum! I hate having sex with him and if you can just take one for the team, I would be thankful. All he does is waste my time!"

I definitely didn't want our husband to hear her. This would kill him. His whole marriage was a lie. So, I agreed and asked her to stop talking about it. I was still confused but not willing to ask more questions. It didn't stop her, she said she hated him and couldn't wait until Eve was eighteen.

She started talking about divorcing him again. I asked her why she hated our Husband so much and all she could say was, "He's a dick." She said our lives would be better when he was gone or when we moved without him.

There it was again, talking about sister and I moving without him. I know she has said this to our Husband a few times, but I think he thought she was just spewing shit out to hurt him.

As I was sitting there with all these thoughts running through my head in silence, sister broke the silence. Out of nowhere she then asked what kind of new car I would want. Sister told me I could pick whatever I wanted, and our Husband couldn't stop her because he wouldn't be there. I walked away confused.

DADDY ISSUES

A few days later, sister was at the hospital with her father, texting me about life. She was telling me how her father couldn't go home after a surgery the doctor said he needed. I suggested she begin contacting nursing homes to find a place for him. She hated her father and there was no way she was going to be able to care for him.

Sister then switched to telling me about the tests she was having. Making things about her as she kept talking, my mind began to drift to a time when her mother had passed away.

I had never heard anyone talk about a parent like sister. It wasn't like she was sad about her mother being found dead in her house alone or the fact she had laid there dead for more than a couple of weeks.

Sister was mad. Not mad about her mother passing but, because it was inconveniencing her and keeping her from her work at the base. She was mad her mother kept books she had read and left a mess in the house. She was mad because she was the only person who was required to clean it up. She was mad because her mother was making her change her schedule and clean up after her.

I listened to her talk about how it was rude to have to jump for her parents because she didn't have time for it. The things she was saying to me sounded the same with her father, as she was ranting about having to be at the hospital because he wasn't being compliant with the nurses and doctors. Sister's hatred for her parents was hurtful.

My head started spinning as she was talking. I'm not sure what she said after she said something along the lines of her father always being an inconvenience. How he was doing this on purpose just to piss her off.

First, I had to hear about how she never cared about her mom and how mad she was having to clean up the mess she left and then about how her father was nothing but an inconvenience to her.

The next thing I knew my text was going off. I lost myself in thoughts of my parents and how much I missed them. My dad hadn't been gone very long and his last words to me were still fresh in my memory. I loved my parents, and I would have done almost anything just to talk to them one more time. My heart was aching over the loss of my parents.

I felt a tear roll down my face as I opened my phone. It was sister sending me a list of things she wanted me to bring to the hospital the next day for her while she sat with her dad. She also sent another telling me how she had told her father she was divorcing our Husband. Why would she tell him that? Her father was sick, and she piled on more for him to worry about. I just didn't understand her motive for telling him.

I walked into the living area and our Husband was sitting on the couch with sister on speaker phone. She told our Husband there were no emergency placements for her father and he couldn't be alone. Our Husband asked her what she would like for him to do. He was always ready to help her. If I had to guess, it was out of fear and not love. He would do what he could to keep her from yelling.

I heard sister say, since Trista was away at college, we could put her father in Trista's room. Sister asked if he and I could go to her father's apartment to pack up a few things for her father to wear and get the room set up for him. She said it would be a few days until she found him a place to go.

When sister arrived back home with her father, she was very pleased to see his room was ready. Her father was a bit confused but was compliant. Sister then made several phone calls to military personnel telling them all the same story.

Sister would say, "I have to take care of my dad, there is no one else. The burden falls on me to make sure he is taken care of."

She would spend several minutes on the phone talking about how she had to do this and that for him and how she was needed there to be in control. She made the whole thing all about her and what she was doing and not doing. Here she was again, making it all about her.

Sister was up early because her father was loud and confused again. She screamed at yelled at her father and told him to get his shit together or go to his fucking room so much throughout the day. I told sister she should be thankful she still had her father and to treasure just hearing his voice. She smirked at me and walked away.

It became more difficult to deal with her father when the sun would go down. He was more difficult and confused this time of day. It was about a week into his stay when he became belligerent. He was throwing things and demanding to go back to Texas. He hadn't lived in Texas in years. It wasn't helping to have sister screaming in his face and also slamming things.

Sister told our Husband her only choice was to call the police because she couldn't get him under control, and he was threatening to kill himself. Our Husband was trying to help and be supportive at the same time. Nothing our Husband did was right, and sister kept yelling at him. All the yelling was upsetting everyone, especially her father. Sister went into the bedroom and called the police.

Her father was taken to the hospital with a police escort. All three of us knew he couldn't stay in the ER and having him at the house was starting to cause issues. Sister was on edge every minute of every day. It didn't matter what anyone did, it was wrong. Sister's anger was turning violent, and I was getting scared.

When sister came back from the hospital with her father for the second time, our Husband had to get back to his base. I cried when he left. I feared sister at this point. She was walking around the house like a time bomb waiting for someone to light her fuse.

Eve was first on her list, I was second. Why I let her get under my skin I'll never figure out, but I did. I told her to stop talking to me and I walked away. I went to my room and called Karma; I needed a friendly voice.

While Karma was on the phone, sister came in and was yelling at me. I told her I needed a few minutes, and she began yelling about her dad. Sister started yelling about how she never wanted her dad in the house and how our Husband was to blame. It was our Husband's fault because he was the one who made sister bring him to the house. She yelled because she told him to not bring her father's things to the house. I was so confused. I was in the room when she told him to bring her father's things and when she made all those phone calls, gloating about how she was doing all the things for him.

Just as I was about to tell her I needed a minute to talk with Karma, sister looked me in my face and told me how she wished her father would hurry up and die. She didn't stop there, she continued with how he would probably pick an inconvenient day to die and fuck everything up for her. I tried so hard to get sister to stop talking because I saw her father standing right behind her. Her father heard every word. My heart sank. Karma was on the phone crying.

Sister turned around and saw her father standing right behind her. She yelled in his face, "I fucking hate you and this is all your fault!"

The look on his face was just total devastation. I cried. I had to hang up with Karma to call our Husband. While on the phone with him, sister came back into the room. She was screaming at me about things, and I had no idea what she was talking about. She then turned and told Eve they had to leave because I was kicking her out of the house.

Sister was angry and referring to a comment I had made a few days before when Eve kicked me. (She was violent a lot, she messed up my left elbow badly and I had to have surgery to fix my right shoulder because of Eve.) (Coming from an abusive relationship, getting hit sometimes triggers my fight or flight response.) This time it was the fight response and body muscle memory kicked in and I accidentally hit her while I was trying to push her away from me after Eve hit me the second or third time. At one point I was on my back trying to push her away from me with my feet. It was a horrible time for me and I'm sure for her. My statement was something to the effect of not feeling safe with Eve being so violent and sister being on edge. Not one time did I ever say I was kicking her out. It was sister's house, not mine. How could I kick someone out of their own house?

I was scared, very scared and had offered to leave. Talking with our Husband on the phone I kept saying I would take Raven and leave. Sister then told anyone who would listen, I was kicking her out of her own house. Sister demanded our Husband find her a place to stay until her dad died or she could push him into a home. I tried talking with sister, but she was completely out of control. Eve was also screaming something I couldn't make out.

I didn't sleep much that night. Flashbacks to when I was married to an abusive man started happening. Sister swinging her arms like she was going to hit someone ran through my mind. I wasn't sure if sister was looking for a severe punishment or attention, but I was scared and sad all at the same time.

Sister, her father and Eve left the following day without a word. I was so confused.

MIXED EMOTIONS

At this point I feel as if sister had abandoned me and all the love and trust we had built. She was telling lies to make things look as if I had done something wrong. I had never kicked her out of her own home, and I never said if she stayed, I would leave. I did tell her I didn't feel safe with Eve alone and I did tell her I wanted to be alone and to leave me in the bedroom. I also offered to leave with Raven until things calmed down.

What was she trying to prove? What was happening? Was this a part of a bigger plan she was working on or was she seriously losing her mind? As I write this, I already know the answer but this day I was swimming in unanswered questions.

Sister was gone for a month. During that month, our Husband and sister were able to find a place for her father to go after he had another procedure. I was then asked to help move his things to the new place so he would have some familiarity when he arrived at the assisted living place.

Sister tells everyone I kicked her out and then asks our Husband to ask me to help with the move. She makes everyone think I am a terrible person and wants me to help her. You all know, I did help. I am not the type of person to let anyone suffer if I can help it. Read that again, "If I can help it."

During this time, it was difficult for me to keep track of Trista and her road to recovery because she was angry about me "kicking her mom out." Sister destroyed so much of what I had built with the girls. For what? To make her look better than me in the eyes of her kids? Who knows.

After we were able to get sister's father into his new place, sister and Eve were to come home. I still had a fear of what Eve would accuse me of to try to get me in trouble. I wouldn't have put it past her to hit herself and call the police to tell them I did it.

When Eve came in, she didn't immediately talk with me. It took a bit, but she finally asked if she could talk to me. I sat and listened to her cry and apologize for her actions. She told me how much she loved me and how she felt like we were family. She admitted to being violent and angry all the time and said she didn't want to be that person. She asked me to help her not be so ugly and again, I couldn't say no.

Either she heard every word I had been telling her the last four years or her acting skills were the best I have ever seen in my life. I loved her like she was my own and she was just dealt a shitty hand in the caring mother game of life. My soft spot for her took over and she stayed with me.

This didn't mean I wasn't scared. I locked my door at night and locked up all my important things so she couldn't destroy them. I also made a call to someone who was aware of Eve's serious issues and let them know she was back in the house and the possibilities of what could happen with her. I also had them document all the things that happened with Eve and sister along with witness statements. I was not going to be hung out to dry.

BACK TO NORMAL

Just as quick as things went crazy, they went back to normal. Everyone home on the weekend with just days until our Husband was to retire. This roller coaster was starting to make me sick. I needed to focus on something good.

April was approaching fast, and we were all preparing for our husband's retirement. I was excited because he was so happy and because house hunting in sister's new assignment was going to be a fun project. She and I could spend time together.

I had no idea how difficult it was to find a place to rent in a large city. As soon as you find one you like, it's gone by the time you copy and paste the link to each other.

This seemed to put a bit of a strain on my loves. So, I talked with them both together and had them talk to one another. I usually had to call a timeout when this happened because sister would get mad and stomp her feet or try to walk out. This time was no different. Sister got up and yelled at our Husband and told him when we were all without a place to live it was his fault. She stormed out the door and slammed it.

Yep! Right back to normal.

I waited a few minutes and walked outside to talk to sister. She threw her arms up in the air and was about to throw a tantrum again. I grabbed her arm as she was on the upswing and shook my head "no." I told her it had been a while since she had been punished and she was about to get a long overdue spanking.

Sister bowed her head and replied her required yes ma'am

response. She knew the girls were going to be gone later in the day for several hours and she also knew to be ready.

While the day went on, sister would ask questions about her punishment. She was asking if her spanking would be worse than the last time she had gotten in trouble. All I continued to tell her was the more she asked the harder it would be. She would giggle and walk away until she could come up with another question to ask.

I got stern with sister at one point and drug her into the bedroom by her arm. I opened the punishment box and pulled out an anal plug. I handed it to sister and told her she was to wear it until I decided to have her stop. When she reached for the lubrication, I slapped her hand. Not today sister, I told her she would have to insert it without assistance. This was punishment, not pleasure.

I went out onto the front porch and sat in one of the two rocking chairs. It was getting closer to early evening and the girls would be leaving soon. Our husband came out to see what I was doing and to talk to me. I loved our talks. They were becoming more frequent and about sister most of the time, but I didn't care. I loved sister and I wanted them both to be happy.

Listening to him ask me what he had done wrong this time or what he said to make her so angry, hurt me so much. He wanted to know what made him such a terrible person to her. This hurt my heart and my soul. I wish I could fix this for him and for her. I just couldn't put my finger on what was causing all her rage.

I decided as the girls were getting ready to leave the house to pour myself a glass of wine. Sister asked for a glass as well. Her request was denied. There is no wine while being punished. I let sister know she had added to her punishment simply by asking for a glass. She smiled and wiggled in her seat. I knew she was adjusting the plug.

When Raven and Eve left for the evening, I wanted to make sure they were gone before I dove into my job of punishing sister for her temper tantrum. She hurt our Husband, I didn't like to see him sad or suffering. This punishment was going to hurt.

I checked my phone, and the girls were far enough away I knew they didn't forget anything, and they weren't coming back until curfew. It was time for sister to get ready.

PAIN IS PLEASURE, PLEASURE IS PAIN

I slammed my crop down on the counter and sister jumped. Our Husband was outside. I pointed the crop to our bedroom, and she bowed her head and walked to the door.

All it took was for her to pause at the door for the first swing to hit her on the back of her legs. Sister let out a scream which she knew was going to get her another swat. I meant business and sister needed to know.

This time as she was preparing herself for punishment, I made her watch as I opened the punishment drawer, she fully stocked with random torture devices. I would pull items out and look at them and put them back. Making her wonder what I was going to use pleased me and scared her. It was a mind fuck game I played with her. She seemed to like it even though she was scared.

I pulled out a hard plastic dog bone with a metal ring on each end. I then pulled out two straps that attached to the dog bone and connected them. This item hurts her mouth and prevents her from talking. The tighter it is the more it hurts. I handed it to her, instructing her to put it on.

She asked about the anal plug, and I hit her with the crop. There is no talking allowed by sister during punishment unless I asked her something. She asked for it by speaking. Sister knows the rules. She broke the rules. The anal plug stayed.

Back to my dog bone. There are a couple of reasons I would make her put it in her mouth and attach the buckle herself. One was simply because it was humiliating for her. There were extra rules with using the bone, one of them was, you also had to bark. The other reason was simply because she would also have some control over how harsh the punishment. I wasn't all bad while punishing her. I let her control how tight the buckle was which controlled the pain in and on her mouth.

As sister hooked the buckle, I watched her tighten the buckle as tight as she could get it. I knew she knew, and she knew I knew. This punishment was going to be like no other. I could see the slight smile on her face and the anticipation.

I picked up my glass of wine and took a sip. I then shoved her face down on the bed. I leaned over and I told her how she should be ashamed of herself. I told her she was bad and mean and she didn't deserve my affection or attention. That's when the crop came down and hit her bare ass, blasting out a sound as if I had hit glass.

Sister arched her back like something was trying to fold her in half. Her squeal sounded like a tiny piglet when a farmer cut its tail. (Farmers used to do this so other pigs wouldn't bite it off later and it would get infected.). I couldn't stop the smile I had on my face thinking about her pain. Our Husband was hurt, and she needed to suffer.

I slammed her ass several times with the crop while the bone was in her mouth. I then remembered her telling me the best sex she had with our Husband even though there were never orgasms was anal. She viewed it as a punishment which made her like it even though it was painful for her.

I took the bone out of her mouth and replaced it with a blindfold over her eyes. I told her not to move or the consequences wouldn't be nice. I walked out of our bedroom to get our Husband. I told him sister was naked, tied up, and

134

blindfolded and wanted to be fucked, in the ass.

Of course, he stood up but was somewhat confused. She had yelled at him and blamed him for everything that had gone wrong and for everything that would go wrong and now she wants an ass fucking? I left out the part where sister didn't know I was out asking him to come in.

As he took a step toward our bedroom, he bent down and grabbed his beer bottle and tipped it. When he finished his beer, he walked into our bedroom. I removed the anal plug for him. Without pause, our Husband shoved the open end of the beer bottle into sister's ass.

She didn't jump as much as I thought she would, and he didn't stop with just one hard shove. As he fucked her with the bottle, I leaned in and told her how she wasn't worthy of a fucking from our Husband.

I grabbed her ponytail and pulled her head back and told her to tell me why she was being punished and why I'm allowing our Husband to give it to her. She whimpered she wasn't worthy of his attention inside or outside the bedroom. How he was a better person than she was and his attention, no matter what kind of attention, was too good for her.

I stopped him and told him I was about to get the belt out to use on her. Remember earlier? Our Husband can't handle physical abuse because of his childhood and his father. He immediately left the room.

Now, it was my turn. I pulled open our closet and pulled out a whip. This whip was my favorite, and I knew how to use it. (Learning a whip of this size takes practice and sister was very insistent and reminded me Raven would have college expenses she could afford but I could not.) When she heard me crack it, her entire body swelled up with goosebumps. She knew what was

135

coming and I knew she was excited about it.

The last time I used this whip, sister used Raven against me. Because sister was so rich, she offered to pay for Raven's prom dress about a year ago in exchange for me using the whip on her. I wasn't good at it then, but sister couldn't wait. I knew I was a disappointment to her because of my lack of understanding of the toy. She told me I needed practice in order to give her the pain she wanted.

I have learned a lot since then. The first time I cracked the whip on her bare skin it was just below her ass cheeks. A small trickle of blood flowed from her thigh. Sister let out a scream in pain, but I could clearly see the pleasure on her face.

I demanded she tell me why she was being punished. I struck her again with the whip. She screamed out then dropped her head. She started to turn her head towards me, but I grabbed her hair and pulled it. I pulled hard enough, sister had to arch her back once again.

Sister mumbled the words, "I upset our Husband."

I cracked the whip again against her soft, pale skin causing it to welt up and slightly bleed a little more. I asked, "What else?" I also made it clear she was to stop mumbling and give me clear answers.

She yelled, "Yes, ma'am!" As the whip hit her again. She then exclaimed, "I am mean to our Husband on purpose because I can be!" She continued with, "I like to see our Husband sad and upset. Seeing him suffer makes me feel better about myself."

Hearing this angered me more. She didn't stop there, she admitted she hates him because the girls like him more, she said she was happier living without him and she lied about it to him weeks before, (I didn't know this) and she said she intentionally picks fights with him just because she knows she will win because he is useless.

Making him not like himself made sister like herself more. I asked her why she didn't like herself and she didn't have an answer. That costs her two cracks of the whip. She was now bleeding more and crying.

I decided to change out the toys. I picked up the belt. Sister asked if I was finished with the whip and began to beg for more from the whip. She said she needed to be punished, and the whip was more painful. She liked the bleeding and the pain. Thinking about this made me think about how she begged for pain before. She likes to suffer and hurt. Why would anyone want this kind of pain? What made her feel like this was a good thing?

I picked up the whip and cracked it repeatedly more than ten times. I had to stop in case the blood was stuck to the end. I didn't want blood on the walls or ceiling. She then begged for the belt. She was bleeding and wanted more.

Even though I was angry, and I felt she was getting what she deserved for hurting our Husband I wanted to stop. I felt it was going too far. I was uncomfortable with how her backside looked and what she was making me do to her. I reached down and wrapped my fingers in her hair and pulled sister off the bed. I drug her into the bathroom.

I made her look at what her backside looked like. As she saw the blood and welts on her ass cheeks and her upper thighs, she also saw a few stray hits to her lower back. I was cringing on the inside looking at what I had done to her.

She smiled at my handiwork telling me she still felt she needed more punishment. I made her stand with her hands behind her back, nose on the wall, and tell me why she needed more punishment.

She began with telling me how she told Eve she didn't have

137

to listen to me or her dad. It seemed to be confession time for sister. All the things she should have been punished for started coming out and she wasn't holding anything back.

She even brought out old things she had previously been punished for, begging to be punished for it again. She brought up how she says things in hopes of upsetting and hurting Eve just to cause chaos, she admitted to cheating on our Husband but this time she said the word, "Again."

Again? Why would she say, "Again" after sister said, "I fucked Dave?" Did she fuck our Husband's main man more than once? Was it before or after that time I caught her in Vegas? She had to have fucked him more than the one time I caught her!

These thoughts were swirling around in my head as she was still talking about her wrongs, and I was still spanking her with the belt. She finally admitted to telling everyone her son-in-law was addicted to porn and was spending all kinds of money on it and how her daughter just shrugs because he tells her it's her fault, he has to watch it. My God she is finally admitting those things I told her were wrong, are wrong.

Maybe sister was right, punishment was working. She was admitting it and acknowledging her wrongs. Finally, she was going to stop causing so much hurt because she knew it was wrong.

As I swung the last swing of the belt and it collided with her red, bloody, bare skin I felt a sigh of relief leave my body. I was going to help sister fix all the things she had done and make this family a calmer, more loving family.

Going to bed that night in our room, our Husband, slept on the side and I in the middle. Sister slept on the side closest to the bathroom and our bedroom door because she felt she may need to get up in the middle of the night for some pain meds. She and

I both smiled as we laid down next to each other.

Sister whispered, "Thank you and I love you for giving me what I needed."

I fell asleep thinking about all the great things we were going to be able to accomplish now that sister wasn't fighting against us.

SOLVING ANOTHER MARITAL PROBLEM

One of the big things my loves fought about was a big van they owned. Sister hated it and our Husband loved it. Sister said there were tons of things wrong with it and she hated it. Hated everything about it.

Our Husband wanted to take it out, use it for a few days and see what all was wrong and try to have it all fixed in time for sister's retirement. He asked me to help by going with him and finding all the issues.

Sister said it was a fantastic idea and our Husband would love to have a few days away with me. I pulled her to the side to talk with her. Sister's father was sick, and we were told his time was limited. He was making less and less sense with each passing day. I reminded her of these things and told her I felt it was a bad idea to leave her. She insisted I go.

I also told her he was telling our Husband's parents and anyone who would listen, how she told him she was divorcing our Husband. She laughed and said her father was senile because of the pain meds and the cancer they found growing in his brain and face.

Sister continued by saying no one was going to believe her father until she and I were gone. By then, it would be too late for our Husband to do anything about its sister said with a slight giggle.

She smiled at me, put her finger up to her lips and said, "SHHHHHHHH."

When our Husband walked into the room, sister said it was settled. I would be going with our Husband in the big van, and she would stay back with her father.

With a huge smile on her face she stated, "Your other wife has been instructed to make a list of all the things wrong with the van and to see if she feels like it will be big enough for the three of us after retirement. I will call if I need something and will keep you updated on my father."

Sister helped me pack up my things for the trip. She talked the whole time about how much fun she and I would have at her new station and reminded me about looking for a new car. She reminded me to keep it secret from our Husband because he was not going and she didn't want him to know yet.

TENNESSEE

A few days later, our Husband and I left for Tennessee. He had made all the plans and I was excited to see what the next few days would bring. I was also hoping I would get some sleep. I was not sleeping well carrying all these secrets and keeping them from our Husband. I didn't keep secrets from sister wife. Why was I required to keep them from our Husband?

It was my job to talk with both. I wanted them to be happy with each other because I loved them both. I needed them to be happy so I could be happy. My loves had to be in love with each other. We were all going to grow old together.

Our husband and I arrived at a campground in Tennessee. I was excited about setting up camp and talking about our future. Our Husband had a way of making me see farther into the future than I had ever thought possible. I could see this made him happy. I could tell when he was genuinely happy and when he painted a smile for others to see.

Camp was set up and a fire was built. I sat by the fire with a drink in my hand waiting for our Husband to sit. We were talking about Eve and how we felt about a decision we all needed to make concerning her.

When he finished giving me his opinion on the matter, I told him I did not agree with how he felt it should be handled. Once said, I could see fear on his face.

He stood up and took a step back from me and said, "I don't want to fight with you."

I looked at him, leaned back in my chair and said, "I am not going to fight with you. I just felt telling you how I feel about it and knowing how you feel, we could talk about it and see if we can find some common ground. This is what a disagreement between adults is supposed to look and sound like."

He looked so confused and asked me if I was going to yell or throw something at him or maybe stomp off screaming. I again had to explain to him I was not doing those things and he could sit back down.

He sat back down, and we were able to talk about what we agreed on and what we were able to compromise about. When it was time for bed that evening, we had come to a compromise we could both agree on and one we felt Eve would be OK with as well.

The rest of the trip was amazing. We went hiking, he put on a wet suit and played in the cold water and took me to see some beautiful waterfalls in the park.

I sent pictures to sister, of our Husband and him playing in the falls, hiking and doing other guy things. She was happy to get them and bragged about how our Husband was so sexy. It made me think back to when she was angry at the third sister and was talking about our husband as if he was a possession. I had to put it out of my mind before our Husband could see the displeasure on my face.

As we continued our trip, we also kept a list of things sister wouldn't like so we could either fix it or figure out how to make it work for her. We loved her and wanted her to be as happy as we were.

Thinking about being with my loves caused me to feel all kinds of joy. I thought about sister and how she would tell me she loves me and remind me how I never had to worry about anyone hurting me again. How she was going to make sure the rest of my life was just as amazing as she felt I was.

I thought about those words all day. Our Husband and I hiked through some great trails, holding hands and talking about the summer trip we were all going to take together.

As he talked, I started regretting the agreement we all (the three of us) had made about the trips over the summer. I started thinking about Eve and sister fighting every five minutes. Both always wanting to be the center of attention all the time. I didn't want to spend an entire summer being the peacemaker between sister and Eve while having to comfort our Husband. Especially not sleeping and hardly eating. All of this was slowly killing me.

I had to call sister. If she loves me as much as she claims she does, she will agree with me and tell him. The three of us have been through so much together and I don't keep secrets from her. I must tell her; I must tell her the secret keeping is making me sick. I'm losing sleep and my anxiety is through the roof. She loves me, she will tell him, and we will all get through this. Because we all love each other.

That evening, I talked with our Husband and told him I couldn't stand secrets and lies. I needed everything out in the open so we could all breathe easier, and I could finally get some sleep. I told him I was going to call sister and talk with her about it.

As I hit the buttons on my phone to call sister all I could think about was how much stronger this will make us. I've been hurting for a long time, and this would make me stronger so I could help them be stronger. Working through issues instead of hiding them would make everyone stronger, together.

She answered and I began to talk. I talked to her about all the secrets we were keeping from our Husband and how I felt they were things we could work through to make everyone's life better. She said she was scared to tell him about Vegas but even more scared to tell him about the biggest lie. The twenty-three-year lies. No orgasms for twenty-three years were his doing. I told her that could be fixed, and I would work with her or both and help with the issue. She agreed and I assured her I would be there every step of the way if she wanted.

She seemed happy to finally be able to get things all out and told me she couldn't wait for me to be home. I could literally feel her love through the phone. Sister was ready to talk, and the secrets were going to be no more. Her mental health would improve, and my physical health would mend.

That night, our Husband and I sat in the van and talked about life in general. I told him I called sister and asked her to talk with him when we got home. I explained again as I had many times before about how much I hate secrets and how they were not just hurting me but everyone in the family one way or another.

I then looked at him and told him I knew about him and the third wife. He knew I knew more than what he had told sister, but he didn't know to what extent. He then finished telling me how he reserved a room for him and the third wife in Dubai. He was going to meet with her, halfway around the world, while they were both deployed and fuck. The room was reserved for a few days, and they had plans to do nothing but fuck the entire time.

I think I may have blanked out for a minute because I could see his mouth moving but I couldn't hear anything. I wasn't even sure I was breathing. Was I breathing? Is this real? I remember him sending me pictures while he was on leave in Dubai. She was with him? Was she the one taking the pictures of him and then watching him send them to me? Wait, was I breathing?

He grabbed me by the shoulders, shook me, and asked if I

was OK. Even as I write this, the thought of him wanting to have sex with the third still hurts. The thought of him fucking her really hurts.

I also don't believe he changed hotels and took tours of the city alone all weekend and didn't fuck her like he told me. Furthermore, I don't believe him when he tells me he didn't try to convince her to move in with all of us. He continued to tell me how he "dodged a bullet" with the third while I sat and watched him lie to me without blinking.

After the third sent the videos of him stroking his cock and seductively calling her name, he apparently tried to convince her to agree to living in a compound with him and his other wives. He assured he would be able to talk myself and sister into going along with his plan. I saw the messages he sent her. I read them more than once and I could still see them clearly. I read so much our Husband had said to her, but I still wanted to fix the relationship.

The pain of betrayal running through my mind was interrupted by a phone text alert. It was sister. Her father had just died, and she was texting us to let us know.

A text? Really? Who calmly sends a text telling someone their father had passed away? I couldn't see my phone because of the tears when my father died, and sister sent a casual text.

Our Husband called her to make sure she was OK. I could hear her on the other end of the line talking about how peaceful it was and how she didn't have to worry about him any longer. No more running back and forth to the nursing home to deal with his refusal to follow the rules.

What I heard was "he won't inconvenience me ever again."

We both let her know we were going to pack up and be home in a few hours. She refused to allow this. She sent a text telling us to enjoy the rest of the trip, finish what we started, and she would be really excited to see us when we returned. I didn't agree but she assured us she would be angry if we cut the trip short because she was perfectly fine. Sister said she hadn't felt this good in quite some time.

Our Husband decided we were staying, and he picked up the conversation we were having before the text, of secrets. I told him I was holding three major household secrets. While I was telling him how they were making me physically not well, I was trying to think of which one to start with.

I don't remember what I started with, I just know I felt like I needed to tell him so he could prepare what he was going to say to sister. The more prepared you are to talk to sister , the more likely it won't escalate to a dangerous level.

When we talked about her cheating, I could see the hurt in his face. He said he would be OK if it wasn't one of three people. When he named those three people all I could do was put my head down because I didn't want to see his hurt. He knew it was one of the three, but I just couldn't tell him.

I told him sisters other secret went back over twenty years. His face went pale. I watched him for a few more seconds before I asked him if he was OK. He teared up and told me he loved his girls, all three of them. They were all very special to him in their own ways.

I was a little confused as to where he was going with this, but I listened to him closely. He began with a story about how he and his "brother" Dave were talking about sister. Dave asked him if he had fucked her yet and he had to be honest and tell him no. Dave asked him what he was waiting for and made it clear he could show our Husband how to fuck sister the right way. He made it sound like he had fucked sister before our Husband did.

He could show him how?

I mean that is kind of rude to say to someone you say you love like a brother but OK. Our Husband looked me straight in the face and asked me to look at Trista and Eve. Tall, looks just like their father and very slender. He then asked me to look at Rebecca. She was short, had a heart condition and looked nothing like him. She did, however, look a bit like Dave he said. He asked me if that was the twenty plus year old secret.

Was Rebecca Dave's child? How had he carried this with him for over twenty years? Was he going to ask her after he finds out it was Dave she fucked in Vegas?

Wait a minute! Hold the fucking phone! Thinking back to the severe spanking she got days before we left for Tennessee, she said, "I'm also getting punished for cheating on our Husband with Dave again."

"I'm not telling him," she said again. "I must keep that secret until I question her. She would tell me, we would organize a plan to fix it and as a throuple, we would work through this and be OK."

I told him after his revelation about Rebecca, it was Dave. I also told him how I caught her and all the events that followed when I caught her. He looked shattered.

I reminded him everyone at some point has a weak moment. Some people are strong enough to walk away and others are not. After talking for a bit, he and I both agreed it was something they would be able to work out, but she would have to tell him first.

When I told him the twenty plus secret was just miscommunications between their bodies, he looked a bit confused. I thought, if I was able to help my body communicate with his body I was fully confident I could help her body communicate with his body . Not having an orgasm with your

148

lover could be fixed. I will be able to help sister with this issue as long as she is willing.

Our Husband was sad she had not communicated this problem before but also agreed with me when I said there was a solution. This made me so happy. Our Husband was willing and open to dealing with these problems and moving forward.

I wasn't sure I could move past his lies or the thought of Rebecca being Dave's child. It was late though, and I laid down so I could at least get a little bit of sleep.

Our Husband had other ideas before what he called "sleepy time." He reached over and rubbed the inside of my thigh. I knew what he wanted, and I was willing to give it to him. This time was a little different, he seemed to be more involved in feelings than just having sex. He was gentle,

For the rest of the time we were gone we talked about life and how we were going to help sister wife when we got home. It was an amazing trip and I felt very hopeful about them moving forward and all of use moving to the capitol area. I was no longer scared of losing one of them or both of them.

Don't get me wrong, I was still a bit scared of sister wife and her angry outbursts but I was the most confident I had been in a while.

RETURNING FROM TENNESSEE

Sister wife greeted us as soon as we pulled into the drive. She was so happy to see us and wanted to hear all about our trip. I was a bit taken back when I saw how cheerful she was.

She was acting as if nothing had happened and it was like any other day. I hugged her and held her until she pulled away and looked at me funny. I told her it was OK to be sad and I was there if she needed a shoulder to cry on.

She laughed and said she really was OK and now that her father was gone the only sad thing is, someone had to clean his apartment and she didn't want it to be her. I obviously volunteered to help because I remembered how she was at her mothers and I did not need a replay of that.

As the day went on, there were typical things that needed to be done but there was also the lingering promise from sister wife to talk to our husband about her secrets.

Thinking about secrets reminded me of our Husband thinking Rebecca belonged to Dave. It was ripping my heart in two. I was praying those words wouldn't come out of her mouth during our conversations.

I'm not sure who initiated the idea of retreating to our bedroom for some conversation but we all three went into our room. I told sister wife I could stay or go depending on what she wanted from me. She asked me to stay.

I stayed and held her hand while she began to talk. She started off talking about her little roll in the hay with Dave. She took all the responsibility for her actions and started to beg for forgiveness. Our Husband looked at her with the kindest of eyes and told her it hurt his feelings but he was willing to talk it out with her and forgive her.

He looked at sister and asked her what else she had to tell him. For some reason this was difficult for her to put into words and for her to admit. She was looking at me for help but I wasn't sure what to say.

I just started talking. I wasn't talking to just one of them, I was talking to both of them. I explained how sometimes it is difficult for couples to find a rhythm when it comes to sex and their bodies. I did what I could to delicately explain how not being satisfied sexually sometimes causes uncomfortable situations and feelings for people.

When talking to sister wife in particular, I explained to her how when it comes to sex, she needed to talk with our Husband about what feels good and what really doesn't do anything. Looking at our Husband, I explained to him how to look for cues to tell him if how he is moving is a good or bad feeling for sister wife.

When our Husband looked at sister wife, he asked her why she never brought this up before and how he could help make this better for her.

Out of nowhere, sister wife jumped up off our bed and began screaming at our Husband. He looked just as confused as I did with her sudden outburst. When she was done screaming at him, she turned her anger on me. Saying her life was over because I made her tell him.

I placed my hand on her shoulder, attempting to calm her. I asked her how I could help and explained to sister that our Husband wasn't angry, just confused. We both wanted to help

151

her and how neither of us were mad.

Her outburst continued and she left the house.

Our Husband and I stood by the door with nothing but confusion written all over our faces. What had just happened? We did everything right and she still blew up.

Sister eventually came back but I feel it was more to harm than it was for good. I was angry with her and I think our Husband was as well. Why was she always so crazy?

I wasn't sure how long I was going to be able to handle her. I had told Trista I would do all I could to keep her parents together but this was becoming more than a job. Sister was making things more difficult as the days grew closer to summer.

No help from sister

Our husband and I went to sister wife's father's apartment to clean it up since he was gone. Sister wife was acting like a two-year-old and I wasn't about to spend the day listening to her.

When we pulled up to the apartment, I was already dreading going in. He wasn't my dad, but since I was the paid help without a paycheck, I knew I had to. Sister would do anything for Raven if I did what she asked. Makes one wonder who was the Dominatrix and who was the Submissive sometimes.

Most of her father's things we threw in the trash. Our husband and sister wife were multi-millionaires and really didn't keep anything. Not really sentimental either. I walked over to the closet and pulled a suitcase out of the bottom. It was heavy which I thought was weird. Our Husband walked over as I was undoing the zipper of the bag.

OK, I now can clearly see where sister wife gets her weird sexual nature. Her father had a suitcase full of XL "outfits" of the female variety. There were stiletto heels in his size along with G-string ladies' panties and some battery-operated butt plugs. Thank God those were clean. I did, however, find something of interest. I went to get a disinfectant wipe and with gloves on, I reached in. There she was, a paddle, with the word "SLUT" cut out backwards. If you hit the skin it would automatically imprint "SLUT" on the skin. Definitely something I didn't know I needed until I saw it. She's mine now.

When our Husband and I were finished we went back home

to work on getting things ready for our girls for the end of the school year and gym year.

With sister upstairs pouting, I was having difficulties concentrating on planning the girl's graduation party and team summer party. Sister wife was supposed to be helping me plan these parties and execute them. Here I am, doing this alone. Why was I so surprised at this turn of events?

Sister was going to be severely punished for this. I will not stand for this type of behavior when there are things that need to be done. The more I worked alone the more I felt I needed to punish her.

I decided to put a list together for the girls to go out and fill. While they were gone, I was going to get sister and let her know I will not allow this behavior.

Walking up the stairs, I made sure to let the buckle of the belt hit each stair. Sister had to know I was coming. When I opened the door to Eve's room where sister had gone, I found her sleeping on the bed.

I grabbed her hair and pulled her off the bed. I looked at the door and sister knew she was to go to our room. I watched her walk down the stairs and into our room. As I walked by the door, I reached out and closed it without saying a word. I left sister wife in the room alone for about thirty minutes. She hated not knowing and that is what she deserved. I had to tell myself this over and over because I was trying to believe it myself.

I wanted her to hurt this time. I wanted not just physical pain for her but emotional pain. I wanted her to suffer. She was causing the girls pain and I wanted her to feel just as bad. No, I wanted her to feel ten times worse.

Our Husband was outside cleaning up the back yard. This made it easy for me to punish sister for her behavior.

I walked into our room and sister was on her knees by the bed with her head and arms resting on the side of the bed frame. She looked so helpless on the outside but the inside was nothing but evil and dark.

I couldn't let her get to me. I had to do this and not just for her but for me.

I told her to stand and get the cream from the bathroom. She started crying and begged me not to use it. I stood there silent. She whimpered all the way into the bathroom and all the way back. When she reached for the gloves to apply it, I sternly said, "No."

Sister wife's crying became louder and I smacked her leg right above the knee with the riding crop. Sister instantly stopped breathing so she wouldn't make noise.

After she applied the cream to her ass, she started to lay face down on the bed. I stopped her by placing the crop, with a swift swing, right on her left breast. Hmmm, that's going to leave a mark. I made her stand.

Having her punishment standing was harder for her. She also deserved this. No bending knees, no steps, no swaying. If she moved, the punishment doubled and what I was about to give her, just one set was going to be harsh.

To make things fun for me I made her count the number of times my riding crop hit her. When she got to nineteen, I made sure I swung it twice as far as the previous nineteen. I could tell she wanted to fall but stood her ground. This wasn't pleasing to me.

I knew exactly what she needed at this point and I this was going to hurt more than her body. I was ready to hurt her to the core.

I walked over to my paddle drawer. Slowly opening it, I

watched sister wife looking at me out of the corner of her eye. I reached in and grabbed the SLUT paddle from her father's house. Her face turned a darker shade of red. Sister was about to be shamed as well.

You could see "SLUT" in bright red on her ass cheeks and her thighs. After several hits and telling her she was a whore I could no longer see the word on her skin. Nothing but red marks, welts and blood were mixed in with the bruises from her last spanking. Not even the blood stopped me from continuing.

With each hit, I would say something else to her to shame her for who she was and what she had done. I made her feel terrible for making me clean up after her dad, I told her what a poor daughter she was to him and I reminded her of things she said to him.

I was surprised our Husband didn't come in. I knew he was outside but I was sure if someone was in the rental next door, they were definitely hearing what was going on in our room. Between me and my raised voice and her screams for mercy someone heard.

Sister wife still had not used the safety word so I wasn't stopping. She wanted more. I was going to give it to her. I decided to stop when the girls pulled up in the driveway. They may have known we were all "together" but they didn't know about this side of things. Today, they weren't going to know either.

I did have one last punishment for sister before she was allowed to shower. When I pulled her up by her hair, I told her to wipe the tears from her face. Just like every other time before, she reached up with her hand and wiped her face. I couldn't help but smile. Just as she was about to ask me what was so funny, her face began to burn from the residue of the cream she had on her hand.

I said nothing to her as I walked out the bedroom door and into the kitchen to get some water. The girls walked in as I was turning on the tv. Eve yelled something about Trista coming home later in the day because her semester was over.

TEAM PARTY

It was a windy day on the beach. There was no way our local base was going to allow us to use the shelter on their beach. There was an incident a few years back where a couple of people died because the shelter was open but the water was closed because of riptides. The party ignored the double red flags and went swimming.

We arrived and yes, it was closed. Our Husband tried all he could to get them to open it while I looked for another venue. One that was available in fifteen minutes for the entire day. About the time I found one, the commander called and was going to let us into the shelter. We decided on a new place, it had a pool.

The venue was the clubhouse in our neighborhood. Our husband went straight to the clubhouse and I ran by the house to tell sister wife we had changed places. That's all it took for her to blow up. I told her she was not allowed down there until she stopped acting like a toddler.

Walking to the car to go back, I stopped and yelled to sister wife to tell her the kids would be back to get some things.

Apparently, we all had to go back to the house for one thing or another. Sister wife started screaming at our husband for who knows what and now Eve wants to attend the party.

I told Eve this was Raven's last team party and she had to respect the fact it was not an "Eve" day. She agreed and went to get her things for the pool. I was hoping I didn't make the wrong choice.

I tried to think of a time we took Eve somewhere and she actually didn't cause a scene. She always had to be the center of attention and Eve would go to great measures to be there. Universal Studios was my favorite. Tons of people walking around, security showed up, people looking at Eve and sister wife as they physically were fighting. I was so embarrassed but realized I was far enough away and no one knew I was with them. People around me were talking. I just shrugged my shoulders and looked at the scene like everyone else. Team party was different. Everyone knew everyone. Please let Eve behave.

I told sister wife if she couldn't get it together not to show up. I was happy when she did show up. It meant she saw how important this day was to me and to Raven.

The day was fun for Raven in a bittersweet kind of way. She would leave for college and have a new team. This was her last time as a leader for her team and she needed this to go smoothly.

While we were cleaning up after the party, sister wife was wearing capris pants on a sunny, hot day. It was just crazy. I walked up behind her and smacked her ass. She jumped and screamed. Then I remembered how hard her punishment was the day before and laughed at her and her pants. Maybe next time she will listen to what she is told and not throw fits. As soon as the thought came across my mind a slight laugh came out.

I knew better. It was only a matter of time before she blew up and scared me to the point of having true fear. Sister wife knew my past and knew how far to push my fear before it turned into terror for me. Why would she do this to me? Did she really need that much control?

My thoughts on Sister wife's sub/dom dilemma

Sister wife claimed to be a submissive but the more I watched her the more I felt she was anything but submissive. She had to control all aspects of my life.

If I needed a medication refill, I had to ask her because she set up an online order page and held the password. She also had all the login information for my doctors on base and if I needed to send them a message for an appointment, sister had to do it.

It was like she had to control all my medical things. She set up my appointments and if I had any tests ran, she stalked my medical pages until the results were in. She would know what was wrong with me before the doctors would call to tell me.

If at any time I had results, she researched what any abnormalities were and called me to tell me the worst-case scenario. She had all kinds of control over me and my medical.

It wasn't just my medical though. She had to control everything in the house. To do this, she had to keep me on edge with what she was going to do next to have me on my toes. She controlled my every decision every day.

I was always on edge. My body was tense all the time and I was constantly waiting for sister to set someone off and make it to where I had to defuse a situation.

My body was suffering the consequences of her behaviors. My back was hurting all the time and my neck and shoulders were also taking a hit. My body is in a constant state of alert. It was feeling all too familiar for me.

The more I thought about it, I felt sister was trying to do this. Not only to me but to everyone in the family. She was slowly killing everyone from the inside out and turning them into who and what she wanted.

I had to start paying closer attention to her and her methods or she was going to destroy everyone. I loved everyone in the house so I had to be careful how to approach this dilemma. I also had to figure out how I was going to get out from under her control.

PROM AND MY LAST STRAW

Prom snuck up on us fast. Raven was so excited to wear the dress sister had gotten for her the year before just before COVID.

Eve on the other hand was mad because she didn't want to wear, the unused dress Trista had in her closet. She demanded her mother get her a new one before prom day. Even though the dress was new and had not been out of the bag it came home in it wasn't good enough.

I decided to stay out of the dress fight. I reminded sister about the budget our Husband had put us on and what we had left for the month. Sister laughed and walked away.

Eve did get a new dress and I asked our Husband to please not say anything. I was already upset due to Eve telling all of us she was not coming home after prom and going to party.

It wasn't the party or not coming home that bothered me, it was her not telling who's party and where. What kind of party and letting us know if she needs a ride if things get out of hand.

I tried to talk to our Husband about this issue and how it could be dangerous for her. I then had to confide in him about the time she had gotten blackout drunk and had no idea how she ended up where she did or what had happened to her while she was out.

I cried while telling him and I could see the hurt in his face for her. I needed him to intervene in her decision making and help her see how dangerous this could be for her. He finally agreed and decided to talk to Eve.

While talking to Eve, our Husband tried to explain to her the dangers of drinking and not being aware of her surroundings. Eve did her typical eye roll and walked away.

I could feel the tears trying to come out so I took several deep breaths as Eve stormed up the stairs yelling about how she wasn't a baby.

Sister wife then showed up wanting to know what was wrong with Eve. Our Husband tried to explain to sister about the conversation and I could see the signs of a blow up coming.

I tried to talk with sister wife and to deescalate her before she got out of control. Just when I was able to calm her down and the three of us talked about what a safe prom night looked like, sister started screaming.

Sister looked me right in the face and screamed, "I don't care what happened to Eve tonight at prom or after! If she gets drunk and arrested or drugged and raped it is her problem not mine and she will just have to deal with it herself!"

Just because Eve got on my last nerve every chance she got, I loved her and didn't want anything to ever happen to her. I saw her potential, need for structure and love and her mother saw a crazed teen who was out of control.

She didn't care what happened to her. Sister said she gave up on Eve years ago and knew she would end up in prison before she was out of her teens anyway.

The more sister talked about Eve the angrier I became. I took a step towards her with my hands clenched. Our Husband stepped in-between us because he could see my anger building.

I looked at sister and said, "That's it! My last straw, I'm done with you. I will not live in this violence and I will not stand her and let you trash the children like you do."

Tears began to roll and I could not stop them. It all came

together at that second for me. I couldn't help sister but I also couldn't let her take me, Raven or the other girls down with her.

I wiped the tears and took a breath. I raised my eyes to meet sister's and said, "If you don't want to mother your children, you know the ones you made clear you never wanted, then I will! I love them and I care about what happens to them. You only care when it draws attention to you!"

I had to walk away. I felt like my heart was going to fall out of my chest. I had to get it together. I had prom hair and pictures to take and the girls needed me to have a smile on my face and it was my job to make sure they had a great experience.

Trista came downstairs looking confused when she saw how red and tear soaked my face was. I couldn't tell her what had happened and what her mother had said because of her past rape. It would kill her to know how little her mother really cared.

I had to think quickly of what I was going to tell her because I knew she was going to ask. Before she had a chance, I looked at her and said, "I'm on a serious struggle bus right now and could use a hug, my baby is going to her senior prom and I'm not handling it well."

She smiled and hugged me. Trista then reminded me how Raven made it clear she was taking me to college with her so it would be fine. We both laughed and went upstairs to help the girls get ready.

I had to make sure this ran smoothly; Raven and Eve were so excited about the night. When all the hair and all the faces were just perfect for them, we took them outside for pictures.

I tried to get sister wife to take pictures with Eve but she refused to come out of our room. I explained that it was about Eve not her and she needed to have these taken with Eve for Eve. Sister wife just turned over in bed and refused to move.

Pictures went smoothly and our Husband made sure to take pictures with both girls. Raven also had friends stop by to have pictures taken with her. They were happy which means I was happy.

Raven showed up at an early hour. I was in the living room watching tv because there was no way I was going to sleep with sister wife. Raven talked about the sunset cruise and the yacht they used for prom. Dinner was apparently OK but she was starving.

While she ate, she talked about the after party and how it was lame. She said it looked like all everyone wanted to do was get drunk, do drugs and have sex. Her words were music to my ears. I loved how she was so careful with her mind and her body.

"I fell asleep on the couch. I was ready to forget about the day," the words said about Eve, and to start focusing on my future without sister wife.

LIFE WITHOUT SISTER WIFE

I was done. There was no way in HELL I was staying with sister and dealing with this abuse. I had that life where someone controlled my every move and I was not about to have it again.

Sister wife was good. She actually made me believe I had a choice in how I lived my life but her smooth, manipulative behaviors sucked me in. I'm not even sure behaviors would be the right word. There are so many things she could be called and I wanted no part of any of it.

At this point I was so angry at myself for allowing her to manipulate me so much. But I would do anything for Raven, up to and including, staying with sister wife until Raven graduated.

I couldn't physically check out but mentally I could. I decided to tell our Husband my feelings. I hoped he would understand but also knew she was his wife and he would go with her. I loved them both but violence was getting in the way and no amount of love I had for our Husband or for sister wife would make me stay and live in fear.

I pulled our Husband aside to talk with him about the decision I had made. As I was explaining it to him, I could see the sadness on his face. I knew he loved me and I loved him enough to tell him it was OK to leave and go with sister. I had a home a few states away and I could go back there.

Our Husband said he understood where I was coming from and asked me not to leave just yet. I asked if Raven and I could stay until she went to college. He agreed and let me know he had not made up his mind what he was going to do.

Sister wife came into the room and looked at both of us. We had already stopped talking at this point but she automatically thought we were talking about her and she blew up.

Sister packed her car and walked out the door yelling, "You won't see me any more."

I wasn't sure what to say about her words. I just knew I didn't want to hear her screaming any more. I was just about to take in a deep cleansing breath to help my body relax. Our Husband sat at the desk in front of his computer asking me about summer plans.

That's when it happened, sister wife flung the front door open and headed straight for me. She threw her hands up in the air and everything she had in her hands went flying. I was terrified. I thought she was going to hit me in the face and my fight or flight kicked in.

I was cornered so I ducked and screamed just like before (when I was married to the cop) and sister knew at that very moment she had fucked up. I laid on the floor in the fetal position, shaking and crying. My head is spinning to the point I may throw up. Sister broke me and she knew it.

Sister threw some ripped pictures of her and Dave at our Husband and continued to yell at him as she walked back out the front door.

Raven came down the stairs and saw what was going on and headed out the front door. Raven told sister she was being childish and needed to stop. Sister screamed at her and threw her glasses off her face.

By the time I was able to pick myself up off the floor and get to the front door to protect Raven, sister was in the front yard stomping her feet and flailing her arms. I looked up to see the tourists from across the street with their phones out. They were aimed at our house so I could only assume they were taking a video at this point.

167

I wanted to go back inside but I couldn't leave Raven out there alone with sister wife. I noticed several people outside taking video. I told Raven to let her throw her fit and we needed to go inside.

Sister wife then threw herself in the ditch in the front yard. I had to laugh and I couldn't stop myself. It was a welcome feeling from the horrific feeling I had just a few minutes earlier. Watching her flop around like a fish out of water was not only entertaining for me but for all the vacationers up and down the street. Raven found no humor in what sister wife was doing.

While sister wife was in the ditch flopping around, I started thinking about the time she flipped out at a Home Owner's Association (HOA) meeting. People in our neighborhood are still passing that video around to people. I wanted to crawl under my chair but we were outside. Everyone there and all those who got the email or text with the video could clearly see I was terribly embarrassed. Still to this day, the locals call her the "crazy lady" or the "psycho lady" of the neighborhood.

When I looked up, sister wife was laying lifeless in the ditch making this noise that sounded like a dying cow. I looked across the street where people still had their phones out and shrugged my shoulders. I went back in the house. I was still shaking from her charging at me in the house.

It took a few minutes for her to realize she didn't have any of us outside as an audience. Usually when sister realizes we just don't care she stops flipping out. She came into the house, grabbed her keys, and left.

She sent a text to let our Husband and I know she would be back for graduation but she would not be staying in the house. She would rather have a hotel room.

GRADUATION DAY

My baby Raven was about to graduate high school and leave the nest. Over the last four years I have listened to sister wife, Eve and Trista tell me all about how I coddled Raven so much she was never going to be able to make it on her own. If I heard anyone saying anything negative today, I was going to turn into sister wife and tell everyone her "crazy" was contagious.

All my kids showed up for the festivities. They were happy to be all together. They don't get along every day but they always come together when it's for a family member and they all love Raven.

I talked with our Husband and let him know I would not be sitting with him or sister wife at graduation. I didn't want to have any issues with anyone and from all my past experiences, sister wife could never do anything in public without throwing a toddler tantrum.

He wasn't happy about not sitting with me but he understood. He was thankful his parents showed up so he wasn't sitting alone with her.

I sat with my older kids away from our Husband and sister. Graduation was amazing. The entire ceremony was absolutely perfect from the time the music started until all the graduates walked out. I couldn't have made it any better.

After graduation, there were so many pictures to be taken. Raven with her siblings, Raven with her friends, Raven alone, so many to be taken. When I look back at them, it makes my heart happy to see us all together. Our Husband even came over and had his picture taken with Raven.

Tears fell and laughs were heard as we walked to the car to go home. Raven was going to a party and would be home later. She told me where it was and who all was going with her. Once again, she assured me she would leave if there were any drugs or alcohol being served.

I turned the corner of a building as we were walking and sister wife was standing about fifteen feet from me lurking in the shadows of the buildings. I almost jumped. She jerked her body in the opposite direction and practically ran to her car.

I saw the look on the older kids' faces and just shrugged my shoulders. "Don't ask" was all I could get out. We talked all the way home about the graduation party we were having for Raven & Eve.

Raven was home early that evening and Eve showed up the next day. This was the second time Eve had gotten so drunk she blacked out and couldn't remember what the party was like. It was also the second time I seemed to be the only person concerned.

I had to stop thinking about it. I had all four of my beautiful children with me and it was time to make sure all my ducks were in a row for the party.

I called and checked with the caterer to make sure the food would be ready for pickup on time. I had a plan for who was doing what the morning of the party and went over it with them. Now it was time to sit back and relax.

I grabbed a glass and bottle of wine and out the back door I went. My oldest daughter passed on the wine because she was pregnant but my son and other daughter joined in. Our Husband joined us later.

I asked about sister wife after everyone else went inside. He said she didn't take any pictures with Eve at graduation and was standoffish the entire time.

That night when our Husband and I went to bed it was quiet in the house. He let out a long sigh. I told him I agreed. We talked about the party the next day a bit more but not about the food or entertainment. We talked about what plan of action we would take not if, but when sister wife would throw a fit and start yelling.

****

After our talk, I rolled to my side to fall asleep. Our Husband had other ideas. He flipped me over and ran his tongue up my inner thigh. He didn't want to talk about anything or anyone, all he wanted was me.

He grabbed my hair and pulled it so my neck was exposed. His bite on my neck was never rough so I didn't fight him. He took his time as he kissed down my chest and to my navel. I knew what was about to happen but I still wasn't fighting it. Just as he let go of my hair, his teeth sank into my ass with force. My gasp was probably louder than it should have been.

Having sex with our Husband sometimes can be laborious and fruitless. There were times I would never have an orgasm but I never faked it either. After the day I just had, I needed the rough sex and to cum hard.

Of course, he is going to cum first. I'm so close, he's going to fall limp on top of me and lay there. I need this, no I have to have it. I grabbed his ass as he came inside me and whispered, "Don't stop."

YES!

GRADUATION PARTY

The morning of the graduation party was really busy and chaotic. I had to shower because I smelled like sex and sweat. All I know is I didn't want anyone to have any reason to be mad.

Everyone was doing what they needed to for the party with the exception of sister wife. Was she really not coming to her own daughter's graduation party? Our Husband was there with his parents and Eve's own mother couldn't show up.

The fun part was making up lies to tell people when they would ask where sister was. I feel like everyone decided to blame one of her fake migraines for the no show of her youngest child's graduation party.

I could see the sadness in her face and it hurt me right down to my core. Sister wife only caring about herself and the fact she wasn't the center of attention.

I had to stop thinking about it because I was getting angry. Why would she intentionally hurt Eve like that? When I looked at our Husband's parents all I could feel from them was judgment.

Why were his parents always looking at me like I had done something? Maybe his mom always looked like that and his dad, I could care less because he beat our Husband while he was growing up.

The graduation party was in full swing so I had to stop dwelling on what his family thought and the fact that sister wife wasn't there.

I looked around and saw a lot of people there for Raven but only Eve's father's parents were there for her. It made me sad. Sad because I had seen her invite list and her posts on social media inviting people.

My mind drifted again to the day Raven heard people at school talking about her. How she smelled bad and how she was nothing but weird. How they avoided her as much as they could and how some of the cheer team would lie to her about going places and blocking her from their stories when they had a party, they kept it a secret from her. It was all just sad and my heart hurt for her. Raven did what she could to protect Eve from others and the hurtful things they said about her even though Eve was terrible to her.

The party went well (for Raven) and in the end, we all enjoyed visiting with one another. Clean-up didn't take long and we all headed back to the house.

SUMMER 2020 THE BEGINNING

This summer started a bit differently than those over the past three years. It was quiet and the girls were happy. We were making plans for the summer trip to celebrate our Husband's retirement.

Sister wife had left the day following graduation and wasn't at the party but she was sending emails to both myself and our Husband. Begging for forgiveness and asking for another chance.

Our Husband continued to state he was not going to make a decision on moving to the next duty station for her until he had time to think. I, on the other hand, had already said I was not going.

I think our Husband was scared to tell her. She could be so dramatic when it came to not getting her way and he was fearful she would not act well.

Sister wife sent an email asking us to fill out a questionnaire on her behaviors. When we asked her why, she told us she was going to use it as a starting point to her therapy.

She had refused therapy for so long I really questioned her motives at this point. I also refused for days to fill it out. I told her I was no longer a part of the equation and she should focus on her relationship with our Husband and her children.

She continued to email and was now texting us both begging for us to talk to her and stay with her. Our Husband finally filled out the questionnaire and checked the boxes. You can see from his answers, he was also very unhappy.

The test had so many questions. When our husband answered the questions it showed he was anxious and angry. He also checked the boxes stating how it was difficult to please her and how he makes her feel insecure. How, no matter how hard he tries, he can't make her happy and disagreeing with her would make him scared and feel as if he was going crazy.

Looking at his answers made me sad for our husband. He was never allowed a voice but was always blamed when things didn't go the way sister wanted them to. How her intimidation and threats made him feel small and worthless as well as fearful of sister. I took the same test and my answers were very similar to our Husband's answers. Along with my answers I also sent her a letter explaining to her all my feelings. I was always honest with her and I told her not to ever ask any questions unless you wanted the honest truth. So, I wrote her a letter.

Sister,

I have spent a lot of time thinking about what I wanted to say to you. Some days I want to tell you to never speak to me again and others I want you to know that even though this is difficult, I still care.

I cannot and I will not live this way. I haven't let anyone into my life in a very long time who knows me the way you do. I feel like you have used and abused that knowledge to gain whatever it was you wanted at the time. You played on my fears and my hopes to manipulate situations, blow them up to be more than what they were and hurt my feelings. When I promised myself I would not let anyone have this kind of control, I meant it. I refuse to live and feel that way.

I also feel as if I must go into protection mode when you are here when it comes to our husband and the girls. At times, you seem to enjoy hurting them just because you want to fight with someone and cause some chaos. The yelling and screaming, blaming anyone in your way for the rant you just went on hurt them so much. I love them all so deeply and would do anything to protect them and care for them.

I will start with Trista (as Rebecca didn't live here, I won't have much to say about her). Trista is one of the kindest, most gentle humans I know. She is so tender hearted and the day you sat in the living room and said you wanted to die over and over again after I had asked you time after time not to hurt her in a way I can't even explain in words. When she comes to me and asks me why you do those things, crying and looking so defeated, I can clearly see she is deeply hurt. The damage has been done but I have hopes you will not continue the abusive behavior with her. I would hope the cycle stops and you will begin to repair the relationship you have with her before it's too late and she walks away. She is such an amazing young lady, and she needs stability, love, and a soft-spoken understanding mother.

Eve… that girl can test anyone. I've watched her manipulate, stir the pot, encourage the yelling, screaming and just all around two-year-old temper tantrum behaviors when it comes to you. In the beginning, it wasn't just you, it was everyone. I began to see some of the reasons she acted this way and I tried so hard (I even begged you) to get you to stop and walk away from her and not give her the audience she wanted until she could ask for it in a polite manner. I explained to you several times all she wanted was attention from you and how you needed to make it positive and not giving it to her by yelling and blaming. You couldn't do it. All she wanted was for you to love her and all you could say to me was it was all our husband's fault she was a "fucking brat" and you didn't want her. You threatened numerous times in front of her and the rest of the house of suicide. I can't imagine what it felt like for her to hear her mom say she was going to kill herself. She's also heard you say other things such as, our husband made me have kids. Just another jab at her for being alive. Her acting out and being so rude and hateful….is pretty much nonexistent when you are not here. It's not her that causes her to be that way, it's you. You and all the hurt you've caused her over the years. When I brought that to your attention, you had everyone to blame but you. You blamed your mom, your dad, our husband, Rebecca (somehow her heart condition made you treat Eve badly?). With you being in another state most days out of the last couple of years, I have seen a side of Eve I didn't know existed. She is a very kind and loving kid. She's fun to be around and her laugh is just so contagious. She has such a light in her soul that is so extraordinary, and you seem to want to kill it. Please don't. Please look at her and then get the help you need to be the person she needs you to be. She loves you so much and all she wants is for you to love her and show her how proud you are to be her mom. You still have a chance with her… PLEASE.

The only thing I really have to say about Rebecca is this…Her eye roll when you start acting out is priceless. She's married now with another whole new family. If you don't change, she has a new family and the only person who will miss out on her is you.

I know Raven isn't biologically yours but there are a couple of things I want you to know. You have done a lot to help her, and I thank you for that. You have also hurt her. She saw all the things that went on here. She cried, sometimes with me, sometimes with Trista and sometimes with Eve. I will never forget her looking at me and saying, please don't ever say that to me…it would make me want to kill myself. (Sorry, you wanted honesty.)

I can't speak for our husband, but I can tell you what I see. I see a man who has gone out of his way constantly to try to make you happy. He puts himself last and seems to ask himself how you feel and why you feel the way you do. He second-guesses his actions, words, and emotions daily with you. He cries more than any man I have ever known. With all that, you still blame him for so many things that are

177

out of his control. You tell him Eve's behaviors are all his fault. Why? Because he chooses his battles with her? Because it takes her two days to clean her room instead of one and he doesn't ride her ass about it? Some things aren't that serious, so he decides not to get all over the top about them. But instead of thanking him for being a father you seem to want to make him feel like he's not doing anything. I have watched you rip that man up and down and he still will ask you how he can help you and make it better. Even now, he questions how he could have done things differently to make you better. I hope one day he realizes (and believes it) he's not responsible for your actions or words. Nothing he has ever done makes him responsible and I hope he can put that guilt behind him. He deserves to be happy, cherished and loved and shouldn't have to work for it or feel guilty about it.

With that being said, I do love and care about you and I hope one day you will also love and care about you, but we can no longer be an "us."

ATTENTION SEEKING 911

After getting all the things she wanted filled out back and the letter I wrote to her she became volatile. She sent messages begging for us to change our minds. I told her mine was made up. Our Husband was still in the process of thinking about it.

She began grasping at anything she could. She made threats and said some hurtful things. I wish she would have just read my letter and took it seriously. Had she done that, I am certain we would have been able to work things out eventually.

She began to text both of us, sending a list of things she has on her plate as far as daily living. She sent a list of contact names and numbers, and why they were important. Our Husband questioned her as to why she was sending them.

He questioned her a few times but I told him she was seeking attention. I explained to our Husband, those who were honestly trying to commit suicide would never tell anyone what they were doing.

From my experience, suicidal people tend to keep things to themselves. They are quiet about their intentions. They definitely have signs if you know what you are looking for. Those who honestly want to die, never tell anyone. They leave notes sometimes but most of the time, suicidal people generally leave everyone guessing as to why they did it.

With sister wife, she was very vocal about suicide. Constantly saying she was going to kill herself. Telling her kids, she was going to kill herself several times in a month's time frame. No matter how many times I told her how much it hurt her girls when she said it, she continued without thought for them or anyone else.

She sent a text telling us all how much she loved us and how she wouldn't bother us any longer. This was her last text according to her.

Approximately ten minutes later when our Husband and I were sitting on the couch talking about what we needed to do, his phone went off. Sister wife had called 911 for herself. Since we didn't jump and call for her, she had to call them for herself.

I knew she was upset, but I also knew she would never kill herself. She had never been able to make a permanent decision alone, she had to have someone else telling her it was the right thing to do.

After sending the text about calling 911, our Husband and I started talking about what his next steps needed to be. I talked with him about the girls and how they needed to hear it from him. He needed to be the one to tell them because sister wife tended to exaggerate so many things when it came to her and what was going on.

She did tell all of us she was dying because she had Alzheimer's like her dad and she had very little time left. Dr. Google told her she had it and she was going to be on her deathbed soon.

We talked about what he would tell them and how he should be careful about their feelings. The girls were not going to take this well and we both knew it.

We also talked about how he should call his mother and his sister. He needed to talk with them and let them know what had happened.

I watched him as he talked with each of them on the phone.

He was hurt. Hurt because they were hurt. I could see it in his face, his expressions and the way he talked with each person.

I could understand where he was coming from. I was also hurting. Not because of her threats and actions but because of the consequences the girls were going to suffer. When the girls were sad, I was sad and so was our Husband.

I hated the fact sister wife didn't take anyone's feelings but her own into consideration. Why would she do this to her girls?

I couldn't protect them from this and neither could he. I've told her several times, her negative actions hurt her kids more than she could imagine. Her answer was always something to the effect of how she never wanted kids in the first place and how our Husband made her have them. I can hear her in my mind telling me how she could care less and how it would be our Husbands problem to clean up.

I don't think she understood the significance of her actions until they made it clear she could have no contact with anyone and she had to be held for seventy-two hours. Then when they transferred sister to a mental health facility that had a contract with the military, shit got real for her.

Unfortunately, sister wife checked herself out against the advice of medical personnel. She told our Husband she was all better and things were clear to her now. She was well and ready for all of us to be together.

Literally less than 24 hours after she was well and all better, she was threatening to drive her car into a tree and kill herself again. This time it was over something to do with her car and the tires. I told our Husband I really didn't want to know.

I was so tired of picking up the pieces of other people's lives that she was tearing apart. I could only imagine what tender hearted Trista was feeling. Sister wife knew threatening to kill herself was one of the things she could seriously hurt Trista with and yet she continued to spout out suicidal ideations any time she could with Trista within earshot.

Hurting anyone and everyone who didn't serve sister or make her the center of attention seemed to be the normal way of life for her. This is why she's never had any close friends. Was I stupid for letting her get so close? What will be the next thing she does to hurt someone?

www.ingramcontent.com/pod-product-compliance
Lightning Source LLC
Chambersburg PA
CBHW022144060526
44654CB00043B/664